"...powerful...bespeaks the deeply pastoral mind of the author... well researched...highly recommended for any parish library."

Brother Donatus Vervoot, NDL
Western Catholic Reporter

"As I read this book I felt a hearty assurance that soon again parishes will regain that renewed confidence which is capable of sustaining whispers of the Risen Christ."

Rev. John F. O'Donnell
The Boston Pilot

"...well worth reading if you are at all interested in the future of Catholicism."

Msgr. Charles Diviney
N.C. News Service

"If I were a pastor, DRE, or parish council officer I would try to get *The Christian Parish* into the hands of as many parishioners as possible."

Russ Faist
Catholic Universe Bulletin

THE CHRISTIAN PARISH

Whispers of the Risen Christ

William J. Bausch

TWENTY-THIRD PUBLICATIONS
P.O. Box 180 Mystic, CT 06355

Other books by William J. Bausch

Storytelling: Imagination and Faith
A New Look at the Sacraments
Pilgrim Church

Trilogy

The Christian Parish: Whispers of the Risen Christ
Ministry: Traditions, Tensions, Transitions
Take Heart, Father: A Hope-Filled Vision for Today's Priest

Fifth printing 1988

Twenty-Third Publications
P.O. Box 180
Mystic CT 06355
(203) 536-2611

ISBN 0-89622-146-6
Library of Congress Catalog Card Number 80-14765

Written in gratitude
on the anniversary of my
twenty-five years as a
minister of Christ and
dedicated to my fellow
ministers, ordained
and nonordained

—June 4, 1980

Contents

Contents

Introduction

Suddenly everyone is beginning to realize that the parish is critical, the basic unit of where it's at, the place where every Catholic starts off. Even with other proposed alternatives and other substructures, the parish will remain for a long time as a central reality in the lives of the people. Too long, however, the parish has suffered from neglect by those in high places and has been treated as a taken-for-granted entity which any warm body could pastor. The parish was just there, while it was thought that the "real" life of the church existed elsewhere—such as in schools or chanceries. Which was like saying that the family and home were just there, but the real and important time was when you were twenty-one—as if the previous twenty years of formation never existed.

Now the leaders are beginning to realize what we practitioners have always known: that the average Catholic (including future bishops) gets his or her first and lasting impressions of "church" from the parish; that it is there that the first incorporation into the Body of Christ takes place; it is there that the daily dramas of life, union, death, and resurrection are celebrated; and it is there that struggles, failures, and reconciliations occur. In short, the parish is finally being seen as the vital and critical hand that first rocks the ecclesiastical cradle, and so its importance can hardly be overestimated.

Much about the parish could be improved, but, as with democracy, there is no workable alternative:

> I can be irritated with my local church, my parish, but I cannot reject it, or give up on it. The territorial parish, I think, is a great invention. It is rooted in the land, in the earth, there is a certain geographical imperative. The geographical parish, I think, is the guarantor (for the most part) of universality in the parish. . . . The territorial parish is a reflection of what southern writers call "a sense of place." The rootedness that was once found in neighborhoods must now be found in parishes. That is why parishes must become a center in people's lives of cultural and recreational undertakings as well as spiritual ones. It is in the parish that, most probably, one experiences community. One learns to draw strength there and to give strength.[1]

Because of official neglect, it is not surprising that little has been written on the parish: some sociological data, biographical writings, and very few theological works. This book tries to fill the gap and hopefully to start a trend. It relies on solid scholarship, yet does not hide personal preferences and prejudices. The book is limited because the author is limited. I will be writing from my own experience and my own study. There are whole areas of which I know little or nothing and before which I stand in admiration and awe. There are the mystiques of the national parishes, the drumming challenges of the inner-city parishes, the soft decay of the old ones. I see and sense these realities at a distance, but I have not entered into their mysteries. The best I can do is what I offer here: suggested patterns and principles that should lead to a creative and successful parish. My desire is that people may be encouraged to see the parish in a new light, know that it can work, that it is a good place to be, to live, and to die.

The book is divided into three parts. Part I gives the general context of where we are today as a religion and explores the factors that have shaped our own peculiar American religious background. This part is essential if we are to get a larger view of where we have come from and therefore where we are going. Part II deals with the four foundations of the creative parish: ministry, spirituality, scope, and social justice. Part III translates these ideals into practice and gives an appendix of various approaches, ideas, and programs.

There is a personal reason for this book appearing at this time. It is my silver jubilee this year. The book is one way that I can thank God for much joy and fulfillment. It is one way I can return something to all those people who have been a part of these twenty-five years and who have inspired, encouraged, and taught me and have happily made me need them more than they need me. I give thanks to them, to my present parish of St. Mary's, Colts Neck, New Jersey which has allowed me both to lead and to follow, to my colleagues in the priesthood who have encouraged me, to Ann DeVizia who once again has masterfully typed the manuscript, to my family, and to my co-workers in the parishes throughout the world.

Note to Introduction

1. Yvonne Goulet, in *To Live God's Word* (Thomas More Press, 1979), pp. 57–58.

PART I

CONTEXT

1. The New Perspective

1

"We are compelled," wrote the thirteenth-century pontiff, Boniface VIII, "by the true faith to believe and hold that there is one, holy, Catholic, and Apostolic Church. This we firmly believe and confess. And outside of this Church there is neither salvation nor the remission of sins. . . . We therefore declare, say, affirm, and announce that for every human creature to be submissive to the Roman Pontiff is absolutely necessary for salvation." Declaring, saying, affirming, and announcing surely left no doubt about the matter of salvation being "absolutely" tied in with being a Catholic. We smile seven centuries later because we know that his Holiness just wrote off the Eskimos, Aborigines, Southern Baptists, and scores of others he never knew existed. And that, of course, takes the edge off his remarks. He, like all of his contemporaries, knew only of Europe, Asia, and some of Africa, and all of their inhabitants were Catholic Christian except for some "infidel" Jews and Moslems, who were already lost causes in general estimation anyway. Therefore, so very few were "outside the Church" as he understood it that the statement does not come off so arrogant and wild as it seems. (Besides, he was really directing it all at King Philip of

France who was being threateningly independent.) Still, the phrase, "outside the Church there is no salvation," going back to St. Cyprian of the third century, has been a terrifying one to many. There comes to mind that strange and fascinating Jewish mystic of our time, Simone Weil, who was so enamored of things Catholic, yet who refused to be baptized for, as she said, "There is an absolutely insurmountable obstacle to the incarnation of Christianity. It is the use of the two little words '*anathema sit*' [let him be outside]. I remain with all those who cannot enter the church . . . on account of those two little words. . . . I have been drawn since childhood to the Catholic faith. I have thought about these things for years with all the intensity of love and attention at my disposal. . . . Now to the extent that [the intensity] grows the thoughts that keep me apart from the church assume ever greater force." She could not comprehend, like so many others, such unwarranted exclusivity.

Now take Pope Boniface's statement and contrast it with another one written a decade or so ago, a statement from Vatican II's *Constitution on the Church in the Modern World.* There the church says, "Since Christ died for all and since all men are, in fact, called to one and the same destiny, which is divine, we must hold that the Holy Spirit offers to all the possibility of being made partners, in a way known only to God, in the paschal mystery."[1] There we have it: an admission that others outside the church indeed are saved. Boniface has been reversed, and the church triumphantly single stands revealed as the church truthfully pluralistic.

What started the dramatic change from Boniface's bull to Vatican II's statement is not mysterious. It was basically a matter of discovery. After the fourteenth century the great world discoveries began and flourished so that by the twentieth century what was laid out for all to see and ponder was a whole planet filled with people not Christian. Moreover, missionaries found that often, especially in the Eastern cultures, high virtue, contemplation, and charity prevailed. Not only that, but there were almost the same spiritual phenomena to be found: prayer, healing, speaking in tongues, ritual, sacrifice, sacred places and objects (sacramentals), symbols, mysticism, and the like. In our time people like Joseph Campbell would write a book called *The Hero With A Thousand Faces* to show us that basically the same themes of fall, redemption, salvation, and saviors prevailed throughout the world. Furthermore, with each passing century it became apparent that Christianity in general and Roman Catholic Christianity in particular, when measured against *all* the people who have ever lived in the last two thousand years, are a distinct minority! Only a comparatively few people of those two millennia were baptized. The same can be said for the estimated seven billion people projected for the year 2000. Therefore it has become increasingly inconceivable that so vast a majority of mankind is lost because they are outside the visible church or are not submissive to the Roman pontiff. It was this realization more than anything else that ultimately led to the declaration of Vatican II.

But from this we move to more personal and critical questions: before people used to ask: "What is the nature of the church?"; now, since salvation is manifestly available outside its corporate boundaries, additional questions are: "Why the church?" "Why belong?" and "Why should I be or remain a Christian in the Roman Catholic tradition?" Theologian Roger Haight catches the dilemma well when he writes:

> One of the presuppositions or principles that has revolutionized ecclesiological understanding is the now common

> one that there *is* salvation outside the church. Not only is the doctrine "No salvation outside the church" wrong, but also, statistically speaking, the common, normal, and "ordinary" way and place of salvation is outside the church up to now, and in the foreseeable future, salvation has been and will be achieved for the vast majority of people without an empirical historical connection with Jesus of Nazareth.... When one passes from a common presupposition that there is no salvation outside the church to the supposition that indeed the "ordinary" way of salvation is outside the church, one must also pass to a fundamentally different understanding of the nature and role of the church.... The working of God's saving grace in all of history is maximized; the necessity and importance of the church is perforce lessened. Rather than being the center, the "kingdom of God" or the "reign of God" in all of history supplants the church as center, and the church becomes relative to or related to the wider and broader workings of God's grace in the world, in religious as well as "secular" history.[2]

He is right. As a result there has to be a lot of redefinitions. It would seem that old notions of church and of Christ must be deepened. It seems that we must reset our focus more on the end-time (eschatology)—that is, the church in relationship to bringing about someday the fullness of God's kingdom, and in this venture having indeed a unique role, but one which does not exclude other authentic religious traditions. That is why some contemporary theologians tend to define the church's mission in terms of God's kingdom, his approaching victory over the powers of darkness. As Gregory Baum says:

> This is done by service and cooperation with others in the humanization of life; this is done through conflict and struggle with others against the forces of evil and oppression;

> and this is done in honest and open dialogue with other religions. . . . The church is universal not in the sense that it is destined to replace all religions and embrace the whole of humanity, but in the sense that its witness to God's coming kingdom has universal meaning and power and can be followed by people everywhere. It is possible for the church therefore to accept religious pluralism not as a concession forced on it by the circumstances of history but joyfully and freely as a manifestation of God's inexhaustible grace.[3]

This indeed is a large mental and emotional adjustment for the average Catholic Christian: to realize that we as a church are, in the words of Frederick Wentz, "a self-conscious minority," surrounded by secular or hostile forces. We are but one type of people suddenly and urgently needing to know who are these other people with whom we brush shoulders: who are the Jews and Muslims, the American Indians, the followers of the Eastern religions, and, most of all, who are we? What does it mean now to be a Catholic church within the authentic multitudes of our global village? It is precisely these kinds of questions that have led Protestant theologian Landon Gilkey to remark that the dilemma facing Catholics is not what form of Catholicism we wish to live with since Vatican II but, more basically, in view of what we have just seen, whether we wish to be Catholic or Christian at all. Questions of identity and commitment must now be faced.

This whole discussion is not merely academic for ultimately it will trickle down from the heights of such theological speculation to bear very practically on the parish. For example, will the authentic parish be a reflection of the old triumphalism, aloof and alone dispensing salvational sacraments to the lucky few or will it be ecumenical and servant-oriented, bearing unique witness along with others on the way to fulfillment? Will its staff be a caste apart or co-workers in the kingdom? Will its interests be self-serving or humanitarian? The new "relocation" of the church in the sphere of the kingdom is more than a debate among theologians: it involves a practical critical decision on the local level as to what Christ might mean here and now to the neighborhood.

2

That troubled poet who took her own life, Anne Sexton, expressed deeply our longing for God. In *The Awful Rowing Toward God*[4] she says,

> and God was there like an island I had not rowed to,
> still ignorant of Him, my arms and my legs worked,
> and I grew, I grew,
> I wore rubies and bought tomatoes
> and now, in my middle age,
> about nineteen in the head I'd say
> I am rowing, I am rowing

As we mull over her haunting lines we're pulled back to the realities discussed in the first section: if we can all row toward God in many boats, why (to use a favorite churchy symbol) take the Bark of Peter? If grace is coextensive with creation why bother with the Catholic church? In all honesty, there are no utterly convincing answers to this outside of faith. All that we wish to share here are impressions, but important ones, on how the church now sees itself in the light of its new context and how we should approach it—and even, why we should stay in it despite alternatives and salvation outside it. These impressions also give us a foundation for a theology of the parish.

Some theologians talk about "anonymous Christians," that is, people of good will who in fact are saved outside the church but in essence not apart from it. Vatican II went so far as to teach that even to deny God's existence did not of itself exclude someone from salvation for what ultimately counts is whether such a person is reaching out for truth and love.[5] Karl Rahner has stated that God creates in us the question long before he offers us an answer on the way of salvation. As Gregory Baum puts it, "Living out of true questions saves us from superficial questions and false perspectives. Living out of the profound question redeems us, even if we never find the answer or lose the answer that made sense to us at one time."[6] Still, all this leaves us with a question as to the role of the Catholic church. Even within the broad context of "salvation for all," what is its mode of being, its authentic stance in a pluralistic world?

There are many approaches to this question but perhaps, following the hint of Vatican II, we might try to see the church as fundamentally a sacrament. There are other models, of course, and Avery Dulles in his deservedly well-read book *Models of the Church* has presented five of them, none of them exclusive, all of them interdependent. But here we pick up on the one model that perhaps gives the best perspective not only to the church at large but to its local expression, the parish. A sacrament, as we all know, is a specific outward sign of an inner reality. So the church is that: it is an outward sign, a concrete symbol of a great inner, spiritual reality, namely, Christ. The church as sacrament is a concrete sign of the presence of Jesus in his redemptive love and grace. The church is, if you will, the incarnation of the Incarnation. The incarnation means to us that God became man in a localized, physical, historical, time-conditioned circumstance. It did not mean that he ignored all those outside Palestine or did not care for them. It means simply that God chose, for reasons of his own, to come into the culture, time, place, and circumstance of first-century Palestine and Judaism to be a sign and a means of salvation for all. He entered constricted geographical, political, and ethnic reality. As such he was to be a living sign, in this time and place, of universal love and salvation. He became a particular person and event within which his universal presence—implicit and hidden in human life—became revealed in its greatest awareness, intensity, and clarity in Jesus. Jesus in turn therefore is not a heavenly exemption to human life; he is, rather, the decisive manifestation of that Presence that exists everywhere. So our conclusion is that since God so chose to be concretized into something as limitedly visible and material as Jesus without losing, so to speak, his universal character, then we can extend this principle to the church.

To express it another way, the church can logically be as historically conditioned and restricted as Jesus himself without losing its essential universal meaning. That is to say, that neither God's coming into Jesus nor Jesus' coming into a visible church exclude salvation for those beyond such visible manifestations. It is just that in entering history he wanted to be a sign, not just an ideal. His incarnation both in body and in church fulfills this. To belong to the church therefore is basically to be a part of a living sign, an enduring sacrament of what God wills for all: loving union and salvation. It is to belong, in John Shea's words, to a "wisdom community" through whose traditions in Jesus we can relate to the divine presence which exists everywhere. It carries no notion at all of elitism, this being church; on the contrary, it carries heavy responsibility to be the best possible sacrament or sign of what Jesus came to be and do for all. As Walbert Buhlmann says:

> All Christians together, in 1966, were only 30.9% of the population of the world, after 2000 years of missionary labors! Predictions are that by the year 2000 Christians will number only 16%. . . . This could be disturbing, but some will ask whether in fact we need large numerical growth, a growth in quantity; perhaps, true to our sacramental nature, we are a small sign of quality—again, like Jesus as one man in one small country. We might be destined to be a biblical "remnant," as Jeremiah spoke of (Jer 40:11) and Isaiah (4:3–4), or the "little flock" of the New Testament (Lk 12:32). After all, redemption means a promise of salvation for all and the church, like Israel, is to be a means of holiness for the rest of mankind; recall God's promise to Abraham: "In you all the nations of the world shall be blessed." The redemption of so many through the sign-church depends, after all, on the mercy of God and not on the success of ecclesiastical forces. This is why the mission of the church is not to bring about the saving of those souls who might otherwise be lost or to try to bring the greatest number of people into the church like some kind of contest. Rather the mission of the church is to build itself up as a sign of salvation for all, and of gaining new witnesses to the grace of God already working in the world. . . . The decisive thing is the power to radiate light.[7]

So, to be a Catholic, to belong to the Catholic church, to be a member of the local parish is to radiate light, to be a participant in the sacramental principle, the incarnation impulse first set in motion by God. It is to be content (peacefully, not grudgingly) with being a minority sign as indeed was Jesus from Nazareth for the sake of all. To be a parishioner is to be a part of the parish and "parishes . . . represent the visible church constituted throughout the world."[8] Yes, salvation exists outside the corporate church but to be church makes one a part of the visible Good News that salvation exists at all. To be a Catholic is to subscribe to William Stringfellow's words: "The religious suppose that only the religious know about God, or care about God, and that God cares only for the religious. The church is not the place where men come to seek God; on the contrary, the church is just the place where men gather to declare that God takes the initiative in seeking men. The church, unlike any religion, exists to be present to the world, and to celebrate in the world and on behalf of the world, God's presence and power and utterance and action in the on-going life of the world."[9]

We can say more. We can say that the church is a sign of stability and clarity. Salvation outside it is more undefined and scattered if you will, but the church is both stable and clear about it. There is no ambiguity and no need to depend on place, circumstance, genius, and leadership. The love of God, given to all indeed and received by many human beings, is rooted in the Christ event which in turn is advertised squarely in the church against which the gates of hell shall not prevail. So even though numerically small when measured over two thousand years, the church remains, among the many world-wide displays of holiness, the visible constant of God's redemptive love in Jesus, the enduring display of his reconciling outreach, and the outward depository of his chosen symbols of reconciliation, atonement, and living hope. This might be what novelist John Updike implied when at a church dedication he said, "That hell, in the sense at least of a profound and desolating absence, exists, I do not doubt; the newspapers give us its daily bulletins. And my sense of things, sentimental I fear, is that wherever a church spire is raised, though dismal slums surround it, this hell is opposed by a rumor of good news, by an irrational confirmation of the plentitude we feel is our birthright." So the church is a catholic (universal) sign beyond all other signs of God's presence, activity (grace), power, and concern. It entered history twenty centuries ago and still endures as a living tradition, a standard, a stable existence on the planet, a linch pin in the ways of salvation evoking words like this from our non-Catholic friends:

> My impression of Catholics? It remains unchanged across the years. Despite their diversity, I see Catholics as a people who find cohesiveness and meaning in the church—and who find it hard to survive without the regular nourishment of worship and sacrament. Priests, cardinals, and popes come and go, sometimes with shattering swiftness. Teachings are modified. But the believing Catholic is linked to a Center which gives stability and continuity, age after age.[10]

Another reason for being in the church is the very human one that all of us, in one way or another, have to belong to something, and no matter what other club, group, or fraternity we choose, we have to admit that belonging to the Roman Catholic church places us in a long, unbroken tradition. We remain in it because it has in fact endured so long (often in the face of external opposition, not to mention its own inner corruption); because it does have a long list of saints, democratically spread among kings, slaves, learned and ignorant, men and women; because (it seems to us) it has more certainties in its sacraments and ministries; because it is international both in principle and actuality; because we feel secure in roots that go back so far to the Jesus of history; because it has that incredible capacity (which we feel can only come from the Spirit) to be always renewed, reformed, and made relevant; because our deflated status in the world historical scene does not negate our responsibility to carry on our traditions, and because we just believe that it has remained faithful in its traditions despite all of our own people's efforts to subvert them. As John Reedy says, "I believe with absolute conviction that God is intimately involved in the affairs and welfare of humanity; I believe that Jesus took our humanity and redeemed us by revealing God to us, and I believe that the Catholic community, with all its faults and foul-ups, is the most faithful means of transmitting the Person and teachings of Jesus to people in different times and places of history."[11] Again, it's the tradition which remains as a faithful sign of what God intends for all.

To join in, to be a part of this tradition, to belong, to be the Catholic church, to be part of this minority sign does therefore have meaning. And, besides, there are very few of us who can in fact go it alone. We need the supportive community we call the church. To believe is to belong. To belong is to believe. We need some sense of affirmation, some indication that what we are about is not odd or that we are playing the fool when we pray or that we are not deluded in the very process of seeking God. We need a communal context for our prayer and our worship. We sense the ring of personal truth in Andrew Greeley's words, "The progressive Catholic is perfectly correct when he says that he can be a good Christian without going to Mass every Sunday, without saying the rosary, without believing everything the pastor tells him. He may also be quite correct when he says that he doesn't particularly need the guidance and teaching of the church, that he makes the important decisions required of him in his daily life by himself. But he would be pathetically and tragically wrong if he thinks he can respond to God's love by himself. The church is quite simply the community of those who accept the message of Jesus and try to support and sustain each other in response to that message."[12] These reflections are not compelling in that they persuade one to enter such a minority church and religion in preference to others, but they do help us to gain perspective. They help us sense, after the disappointment of learning that we are not the whole world, a new role, an identity as sign, as pilgrims (to use another of Vatican II's descriptions) marching through space and time with the Good News, not forbidding its reflections (Lk 9:49), but rejoicing that God is greater than his signs and yet feeling an innate necessity for existing as church to give witness to the presence of the Lord Jesus. To be a part of that is quite glorious enough.

To have come to this understanding helps us to come to terms with a whole new emphasis on all levels. For example, old teaching that saw Christianity in general and the Catholic church in particular as sole universal and only authentic means of salvation has been at the bottom of the colonial invasion of America, Africa, and Asia—as the Third World angrily reminds us. After all, if the Christian people consider themselves as situated at the center of world history and that therefore the rest of the world has meaning only in so far as it related to such a center, then it follows that the white man's Christian conquest of the continents is regarded as God's providential design to prepare the spread of the Christian gospel. Such thinking, as we shall see in the next chapter, was behind the founding of our own country. Now, however, we see ourselves without colonial and imperial motifs, but rather with a more authentic religious vision. And we see others as not untouched by God's grace:

> Christianity, then, is not to be taken exclusively as the one, unique, true religion, like the sun around which all the rest turn. Before and alongside Christianity there are and have been religions with their own "revelations." Thus, we need to study the religious phenomenon itself. Within this general

> phenomenon, Christianity represents a particular and unique form, being the ground . . . on which light and warmth . . . have engendered a life which is especially varied and flourishing. This conception does not depreciate the uniqueness of the salvific action effected by Christ but, on the contrary, accentuates it; for it does not merely confer a preeminence on the church he founded but also relates to the event of Christ all the other religions in God's salvific plan. . . . Today, as in the beginning, there exists no name under heaven through which we can attain salvation (Acts 4:12) except that of Jesus Christ; he, however, is already present and active in all religions before the arrival of the missionary.[13]

To the extent that we now hold this vision we cannot demand that the peoples of the globe renounce all previous religious experience in order to join us. We cannot present ourselves as saying either come in and be saved or stay outside and be damned. Jesus himself did not demand a break from the synagogue. His church therefore must accordingly present itself not as having the only and sole key to heaven but as an assembly that recognizes the truth in others. The church in fact can be the cause of the unveiling of the mystery of God hidden in all religions of the world.

It is interesting to see this view expressed in modern missionary theology. One mission magazine carefully reflects the new view of church as sacrament-sign and the way that the missions are now operating when it writes:

> Meanwhile the concept of mission itself has been evolving almost as fast as technological advancements. What before was seen as the need to "save souls" and "ransom pagan babies" is changing to a greater emphasis on "service" and less preoccupation with "conversion." . . . The emphasis must be

> in terms of the kingdom of God already here and to be fully realized at Christ's second coming, as the scriptures reveal. In this context we can no longer think of mission as "bringing Christ" to peoples; rather it is helping ourselves and others know and appreciate the Risen Christ already present in his kingdom. . . . Our mission is to see that this and succeeding generations realize a more just and moral political, social and economic order. . . ."[14]

All these notions give us a "flavor" about what the local parish should be; that, for example, efforts at evangelization should not be merely "bringing in" the vast unchurched, but bringing them into something. That is, to introduce them into lived charity and justice and the felt presence of Christ. It tells the parish, this new concept, that while the church is basically missionary and will always be, conversion efforts are less pulling people in by hard-sell methods as drawing them by an obvious spirit, by being such a sign of concern, peace, and tolerance that the God revealed in the Jesus who would not reject the Phoenician women's wit will be obvious to the city or suburban dweller's wisdom.

3

We might quickly bring to a close our new positioning or understanding of the church by two final allied thoughts. The first is that if I am persuaded that it is worthwhile to be in (stay in) the church because the world needs a powerful sign today more than ever of Saving Presence, I have a question: Is the Bark of Peter sinking? If so, who wants to be a part of that? We look around and all seems to be confusion and disarray. Should we jump off? In the next chapter we shall try to see that, historically, our disarray is another creative phase, and there are many good signs of creativity and growth although a leveling-out may not come for another decade or two. Yes, there have been many who have left, some noisy, press-conference-calling few, and a few others who make a career out of being ex-Catholics. Most others who have left, like the Arabs in the poem, have simply folded their tents of allegiance and quietly stolen away. Still, those who in fact have left remain a small minority in the American church. Priests have left in force but there are still over fifty thousand of them serving (though the vocation crisis is critical). Tens of thousands of sisters have left but the directory still lists almost a hundred thirty thousand serving, and there are still almost fifty million Catholics in our land. Those who are staying these days are staying voluntarily, and many are sharing in the evolution of both greater lay participation and deeper spirituality. The Catholic church is far from a lost cause.

Secondly, those who elect to stay in the church know that they stay in an incarnational church—which is to say, a church as an assembly, not of angels, but of human beings fully susceptible to frailty and error and sin. I think it was Andrew Greeley who made the crack that if you ever find the perfect church, then by all means join it. Of course, it won't be perfect after that. "Institutional" religion is under attack but, realistically, there is no other way. We all, in all phases of our existence, institutionalize or die. Two different people catch the good sense of this and I would close this chapter with words from both of them, words worth pondering. The first is from a Presbyterian minister who wrote a lovely book on the rosary (another sign of the times!). He says in that book:

> Institutional religion will always exasperate us because it is carried in the words and deeds of inadequate and sinful human beings. Nevertheless, there is no other way of knowing that Christ is risen and really present in this our life than in the only group that believes this and exists to hold this belief before the world. . . . People who attempt to learn Christianity while rejecting institutional religion develop impoverishments and distortions in their spiritual life which are clearly traceable to this rejection. Baron von Hügel put first among these a certain incompleteness in one's humility when it is exercised before God alone, without recognition of my need of other human beings, particularly those who are wiser and better than I, and without recognition of my need of a training and discipline framed by others and by the presence of others. Two familiar dangers dog the footsteps of those who attempt to go it alone, the tendency to settle for a moralistic, "Golden Rule," type of inchoate religion, and the likelihood of intellectual superiority, particularly among the educated.
>
> Without organization, without the church, the Christian faith must necessarily be left to the private interest of individuals who may easily grow bored with looking for God and may never care whether others find him or not. Its prospects then would not interest any insurance company. This is not to say that there is anything sacrosanct about any of the administration or intellectual forms of the church which is by definition always under the mercy and judgment of God, always in part usable, always needing reform.[15]

The last statement is from that prophetic and venerable teacher of the faith, Frank Sheed. When he hears people give all kinds of reasons for leaving the "Institutional" church because of its faults and shortcomings, he reminds them of ancient Israel. The Chosen People from what we read in the prophets were often in worse condition than the Catholic church, and their prophets were severe and harsh critics; yet it never occurred to any of them or the holiest of Jews to leave it. However evil the administration, they knew they were still the People of God. So, Sheed says, with the church:

> We are not baptized into the hierarchy, do not receive the cardinals sacramentally, will not spend eternity in the beatific vision of the pope. St. John Fisher could say in a public sermon, "If the pope will not reform the curia, God will": a couple of years later he laid his head on Henry VIII's block for papal supremacy, followed to the same block by Thomas More, who had spent his youth under the Borgia pope, Alexander VI, lived his early manhood under the Medici pope, Leo X, and died for papal supremacy under Clement VII, as time-serving a pope as Rome ever had.
>
> Christ *is* the point. I myself admire the present pope, Paul VI; but even if I criticized him as harshly as some do, even if his successor proved to be as bad as some of those who have gone before, even if I sometimes find the church as I have to live in it a pain in the neck, I should still say that nothing a pope could do or say would make me wish to leave the church, although I might well wish that *he* would. Israel, through its best periods as through its worst, preserved the truth of God's Oneness in a world swarming with gods and the sense of God's majesty in a world sick with its own pride. So with the church. Under the worst administration . . . we could still learn Christ's truth, receive his life in the sacraments, be in union with him to the limit of our willingness. In awareness of Christ, I can know the church as his Mystical Body. And we must not make our judgments by the neck's sensitivity to pain![16]

So, here we are: members of a church, not a majority corporation as we thought before, not as the Bark of Peter riding across the world's oceans frantically pulling people aboard lest they be lost and feeling troubled in our hearts that those who did not make it will perish forever in the depths (especially dear non-Catholic friends and relatives). We are no longer that citadel on the hill to which all must make their way at peril of being consigned eternally to the darkness outside. We no longer have emblazoned over our doors, "Outside the church there is no salvation." No longer—to bring it down to the practicalities of our topic—a Catholic parish seeking to drag in others, a small rowboat sent out from the bark to rescue our neighbors (who seem pretty nice people but, alas, must be counted as lost). We are no longer, in a blatant sense, "saving the souls" of our tailor and butcher or "ransoming" the unchurched pagan, the Jew and the ever-increasing Muslim with a now-or-never sense. As a parish we are to be a particular sign of the universal presence of the Risen Lord. As a sign-parish we are challenged to grow in such holiness, to live so righteously and to hunger for such social justice that we will compel (evangelize) all others to see by our light, to know by our knowledge (faith), and to love with our love, and, hopefully, to join us in the corporate celebration of the theme that both holds us together and gives us our identity: "Jesus Christ is Lord!"

And for those who won't or can't join there is no anger, hatred, or pessimistic pity. Instead there is resonance, respect, and ultimate hope for, once again in the words of Vatican II: "Since Christ died for all and since all men are, in fact, called to one and the same destiny, which is divine, we must hold that the Holy Spirit offers to all the possibility of being made partners, in a way known only to God, in the paschal mystery."

Notes for Chapter 1

1. *Constitution on the Church in the Modern World,* No. 22.
2. Roger Haight, S.J., "Mission: The Symbol for Understand-

ing the Church Today," in *Why the Church?* ed. Walter J. Burghardt, S.J. and William G. Thompson, S.J. (Paulist Press, 1976), pp. 85–86. See also the interesting book, *Christian Faith in a Religiously Plural World,* ed. Donald Dawe and John Carman (Orbis Books, 1979).

3. Gregory Baum, *The Social Imperative* (Paulist Press, 1979), p. 56. Note also Vatican II's saying that the church of Christ "subsists" in the Catholic church implying a distinction between them. See William J. Bausch, *Positioning* (Fides/Claretian, 1975), chapter 9. For a look into anti-Judaism built into church theology by a Jewish convert to Catholicism see Charlotte Klein, *Anti-Judaism in Christian Theology* (Fortress Press, 1978).

4. Anne Sexton, *The Awful Rowing Toward God* (Houghton Mifflin, 1975).

5. *Lumen Gentium.* No, 16.

6. Baum, *Social Imperative,* p. 48.

7. Walbert Buhlmann, *The Coming of the Third Church* (Orbis Books, 1978).

8. *Decree on the Liturgy,* No. 42.

9. Quoted in James C. Fenhagen, *Mutual Ministry* (Seabury Press, 1977), p. 12. See also Hans Miessen, "Christianity and Other Religions," *Theology Digest* 27, No. 2 (Summer 1979) pp. 121 ff.

10. Quoted in *US Catholic* (May 1979).

11. *A. D. Correspondence* (March 24, 1979).

12. Andrew M. Greeley, *The New Agenda* (Doubleday, 1973), p. 252.

13. Buhlmann, *Coming of the Third Church.*

14. *Maryknoll* (June 1979). For intriguing and interesting insights on the missions see Vincent J. Donovan, *Christianity Rediscovered* (Fides/Claretian, 1978) and Walbert Buhlmann, *The Missions on Trial* (Orbis Books, 1979).

15. J. Neville Ward, *Five For Sorrow, Ten For Joy* (Doubleday, 1973), p. 48.

16. Frank Sheed, *Christ in Eclipse* (Sheed, Andrews and McMeel, 1978), pp. 6–7.

2. The Soul of a Church

1

In centuries past foreigners to our shores would observe that we are a "nation with the soul of a church." Alex de Tocqueville, that sympathetic French visitor of the early nineteenth century, made a similar remark. He wrote that in his opinion there was "no country in the world where the Christian religion retains greater influence over the souls of men than in America."[1] The unfortunate thing is that the average American Catholic (or citizen of any persuasion) does not fully appreciate the import of these words and why they are so accurate. Not appreciating these words, we consequently find it difficult to get a context of our own times. I mean that there are many confusing, creative, and distressful things happening in our religious lives today that could be properly seen in historical perspective if only we knew that perspective. But not knowing our national origins and the deep, ingrained religious rhythms of our country we sense no organic tradition from which to draw insight, solutions, or even comfort for ourselves in our present crisis. Without a feel for our national past we have no way of assessing what our parishes are about or how they might regroup themselves in creative response. So, in this chapter we must briefly look at where we have come from as a nation, how we acquired that "soul of a church" and how we might get a grip on our current parochial malaise.

The first truism we should grasp is that, in Garry Wills' words, "America was born a God-obsessed nation, and continues to be one."[2] This obsession began in postreformation Europe. We might recall that Christianity at that time split and resplit countless times. There were always those who felt that the original reformers did not go far enough, those who dissented from the dissenters. Such radicals went by the names of Anabaptists, Hutterites (who wound up in this country in South Dakota), the Unitarians (to be strong in Boston), the Quakers (who settled in Pennsylvania), the Mennonites (the Amish in Pennsylvania), the Disciples of Christ, the Plymouth Brethren, and literally hundreds of other sects. While disagreeing on some point of doctrine or scriptural interpretation among themselves which forced them to split, they were all against the established religions of their various countries.

England is our particular interest. That nation went from Roman Catholicism to Anglicanism in a few decades, the latter eventually being made the state religion. But radical groups, like the Puritans were not pleased with an Anglicanism that kept too much liturgical baggage from the Roman Catholic church, had a hierarchy (as opposed to the priesthood of all), a standard Book of Common Prayer (as opposed to the inspiration of the Spirit), and an ordained clergy. Later, when under William of Orange who had toppled James II, the rule was passed that only a Protestant could ever sit on the throne of England and also that the teeming religious minorities of the land had to subscribe to certain religious articles offensive to them under pain of persecution and death, then many fled. This included the Puritans. Some of them went to Holland while others boarded the *Mayflower* for the New World.

The Puritans and other like-minded minorities, such as the very influential Scottish Presbyterians, gave to this nation its "soul." First of all, they and all other Englishmen, brought with them a firm conviction that they were the superior bearers of truth and culture. The widely circulated manuscript of one Richard Hakluyt to Queen Elizabeth in 1584 for example argued that sophisticated Englishmen should bring the gospel to the simple natives of America. The first charter for Virginia emphasized the importance of propagating the faith. So it was not accidental therefore that the first shipload of colonists to arrive in Jamestown in 1607 had a clergyman with it or that in 1609 the Virginia Company of London set forth as the first of its purposes to preach to and baptize into the Christian religion "a number of poore and miserable soules" or that the Church of England was quickly established as the state religion in Virginia in 1619. Secondly, they brought a fierce, Calvinistic coloring, the teaching that only certain people were predestined for salvation, and this itself was in fact a gracious favor by God. After all, his unspeakable holiness and firm justice rightly condemns all intrinsically corrupt men. They are irredeemable sinners by nature. The only thing a person could do was lead a pious and devout life , work hard, practice self-control, have respect for one's betters, and strictly observe God's laws—and even these were only possible indications, outward hints, that one might be so numbered among the elect. Wealth became one tangible sign of God's favor, for it resulted from the hard work which in turn was a sign of piety. We are all familiar with Max Weber's famous thesis that Protestantism therefore lay at the root of our capitalist system with its ethic of hard work, thrift, and wealth. This Protestant ethic is carefully enshrined in all those banks and brokeridge houses over twenty-five years old which exude the distinct aura of temple trappings.

As against the state and church control of the mother countries, the first settlers tended to be individuals and geared to family groupings answerable to no church, only to a higher power. They broke the old medieval pattern of a corporate ethic in favor of rugged individualism. They were strict in raising their children. This is not surprising for it was a logical outgrowth of how they viewed their heavenly Father. Their children stood to them as they did to God. So obedience and self-control were the unyielding requirements of a child who was born in sin and lived in sin. Even infants, they said, were expected to "cry softly" in order to have their wayward will broken at an early age. They were a bible people as opposed to a clergy or institution people. This would help them someday to make the transition to the separation of church and state. Moreover, themselves a minority they could abide the religious toleration of others—with certain exceptions, of course, such as "papists" beholden to the "Whore of Rome." Anti-Catholicism came with the ascendency of the Protestant consensus. In time, of course, as so many other minorities flooded the shores of the New World, doctrine became less and less important and instead the Calvinistic moral presumptions prevailed (which were strong enough to topple the polygamy of the Mormons while allowing their doctrinal novelties. We have strong echoes today in questions of gambling and drink).

Finally, and most importantly, they brought to this country or discovered in it (so they felt) the land of the kingdom of God. In time the early settlers began to perceive that this was the land where in fact God's perfect kingdom could take hold. They just knew that God had given them this wild country to tame and bring to Christian perfection. America was to be God's experiment and model. More and more, as they overcame terrible hardships and met with success, it was evident that God was blessing them. America was clearly a living covenant between them and God. They were at last a free people in a free land, in the very kingdom of God. No pope, no king, no Parliament would ever control their lives. They would do what they would do voluntarily. They would marry for love not policy. They would take part in their township meetings and rule by common consent as a People of God. They would hasten the millennium for it would take place in their new country. And, from the New World, they would return the favor and go back and save Europe and Asia. "America," proclaimed the greatest clergyman of them all, Jonathan Edwards, "has received the true religion of the old continent; the church of ancient times had been there, and Christ is from thence; but that there may be an equality, and inasmuch as that continent has crucified Christ, they shall not have the honor of communicating religion in its most glorious state to us, but we to them. . . ."

This pervasive and founding "God-sense" is what we must grasp not only to see our roots but also to understand the dynamic of the several great religious revivals from the beginning to the present moment which we shall shortly investigate. We have to understand that America was established in the firm conviction that it was the New Israel, the place of paradise. Even the New England names give us a clue to the (biblical) mentality: New Providence, New Haven, Salem (short for Jerusalem), New Hope, and so on. Nathaniel Hawthorne tells us that the Puritans at first did not plan to have either prisons or cemeteries feeling that, in the land of perfection, they would have need of neither. America, therefore, from the start was a religiously covenantal nation radically shaped in the Protestant (Calvinistic) mold. With accuracy does historian Sydney Ahlstrom speak of American history as an "uncritical Protestant celebration" and H. Richard Niebuhr proclaim that "Protestantism is America's only natural religion." Both are reflecting Jonathan Edwards's description of the New World as "the principle kingdom of the Reformation." Indeed America was a place of clear and "manifest destiny." From its God-given abundance all blessings would accrue to the rest of the world. That such foundational God-pervasiveness persists and that such core religiosity endures show up continuously in the Gallup poles, in our patriotic songs, in the "In God We Trust" on our coins and, in tamer forms, in the obligatory presence of a clergyman at every official function from the opening of Congress to the first day of Little League.

2

In such a climate it is not surprising to find religious revivalism as a rather constant phenomenon in our country, and they should interest us because we are going through one right now. They arise from the grass roots, beginning with the heightening of religious feeling in an individual or a small group who then seek to affect others in the same way. Revivals are democratic in that they include women and children (unlike, notice, the official ministries). They stress the "felt" and "lived" character of personal conversion and individuals so happily graced are apt to ask throughout the centuries "Are you saved?" or "Are you converted?" and in time, "Have you been baptized in the Spirit?" or "Are you charismatic?" It is also important that one's conversion be recognized by others of the assembly. Frequently indicators of this were manifestation of tears or even convulsions. One of the greatest revivalists, Charles Finney, describes the revival:

> These assemblies are made up for the most part of plain, passionate sermons to which the audience responded with wailing, sobs, and cries.... Each one raised his voice in anguish: there a sinner, overwhelmed by his guilt, asked pardon of God; there another, relieved of the burden of his sins, gave thanks to the divine mercy; elsewhere Christians exhorted their as yet unconverted relatives and friends to repent.... One man, driven by the obsessions of an awakened conscience, tried to flee the camp, and soon fell, stopped short by the sovereign hand of God. Another passed, almost without transition, from blasphemy to prayers. From the midst of all this disturbance rose isolated groups of chanting of an incomparable sweetness, the natural expression of renewed sentiments.[3]

There were remarkable conversions, dramatic turnabouts and quiet surrenders along with the more obvious excesses which caused even Finney to admit "One of the things which definitely prevents people from desiring religious renewal and working towards it is the fact of the excesses or abuses which have sometimes accompanied strong religious arousal."

Our interest in recurrent American revivalism is more in the elements that cause and define them, more in the sociological, historical perspectives of the movement. The reason is that we hope to get a context to measure our own current revival and, as a result, the proper reaction of the parish. We shall use the term revival and awakening—the old term in books—interchangeably. Quite artificially we identify five basic elements of the revival: cultural distortion, confusion/guilt, therapists (revivalists), introspection, and synthesis. That classification sounds very esoteric but behind it are really uncomplicated notions.

First there is distortion. This means that the realities of everyday life begin to separate from the conventional political, economic, or religious ideals. Things as they really are (or are becoming) and things as they are officially said to be are flagrantly growing apart. Social realities grow beyond the old containments, institutions are not seen as meeting the needs of people, schools can't handle the kids, marriages fail, police are incompetent, the government is untrustworthy—all these and similar things are distorting events which cause people to grow confused, angry, and perhaps even violent. A root change is due, a great revival (awakening) is in the making. Distortion is its first step.

> A great awakening occurs . . . when a society finds that its day-to-day behavior has deviated so far from the accepted (traditional) norms that neither individuals nor large groups can honestly (consistently) sustain the common set of religious understandings by which they believe (have been taught) they should act. When parents can no longer adequately guide their own lives or their children's, when schools and churches provide conflicting ethical guidelines for economic and political behavior, and when courts impose sanctions upon acts commonly recognized as necessary (or accepted) deviations from the old rules, then a period of cultural disorientation results. Then leaders lose their authority and institutions the respect essential for their effective operation. Then men begin to doubt their sense and their sanity and to search about for new gods, new ways to perceive and comprehend the power that guides the universe. If they are lucky, they will find leaders able to articulate a new

> accommodation with "reality," a new sense of reality, of identity, and of self-confidence, and, above all, a revision of their institutional structure that will return daily life to regularity and order.[4]

We may be quick to recognize our own times in this description and we would be right; but we should not forget that the description fits all the revivals of the past as well.

Secondly, there is confusion/guilt as an element of a revival in the making. This results, as we indicated, when the way we were morally raised is brought into conflict with the way things are accepted now. There is confusion and guilt in deviating from some social norm, from faith itself. We feel that we are violating the covenant, the moral law. When we in fact begin to lose faith in our institutions and even our churches we feel guilt about that. In modern times, think of those you know who no longer go to church or who have left the church. They can run the gamut from those shocked by rapid and unexplained changes in the church and so harbor a deep sense of betrayal to those put off by *Humanae Vitae,* feeling that forbidding birth control in this day and age is such a distortion of reality (since Catholics seem to use birth control in the same proportion as the rest of the population) that they must break away. Often in both cases there is lingering guilt. In any case there surely is, at the beginning, considerable confusion, a sense of losing one's moorings.

Thirdly, in the process of working things out there arises, necessarily so, therapies and therapists. The therapies are the revival meetings themselves, therapeutic gatherings that can help slough off the past or renew one's sense of order, harmony and inner peace. It moves (converts) people to more relevant and more functional ways of coping. Such revivals range, as we shall see, from the old Methodist tent meetings or the Baptist under-the-tree gatherings to the present day charismatic rallies at baseball stadiums. Along with the mediating revivalistic therapies are, of course, the therapists. These arise from grass-roots people and symbolize their needs and lead them to conversion. They range from George Whitefield, Billy Sunday, Charles Finney, and Dwight Moody of the past to Oral Roberts, Billy Graham, and Francis McNutt of today. Such gifted and talented leaders do not become the object of salvation. They instead focus the issues and catalyze the conversion experience to another. They do not preach a new religion; they merely point to the untapped realizations in the old (as, for example, when the group in Topeka, Kansas in 1900 wondered why no one ever spoke in tongues any more for it was clearly in scripture: that wonderment and what followed began the Pentecostal movement). The leader does gather disciples, usually younger, who join either in formal religious organizations or in informal groups, communes, and experimentations which might range anywhere from prayer groups and covenant communities to weekly bible meetings. Sometimes, we know, such experimentations can be destructive as in the case of unbalanced cults. Each movement, it seems, has its underside of the occult, magic, heavy drug use, and suicide pacts.

The fourth element of a revival is a turning inward. The reason for this is that people have found their religious institutions powerless to help, direct, or enlighten them in the current period of confusion. Often the institutions themselves or their representatives give contradictory advice. Every modern Catholic knows, for example, how parish can differ from parish and one priest's advice from another. The vertical "up-there" God of the mainline churches seems less powerful, more remote, certainly not so reassuring anymore. As the formalized ritual of the established churches becomes less and less satisfying, people tend to seek him inside: in nature, in the flowers, deep within themselves. The transcendent God becomes immanent once more. People become more introspectively spiritual and look for a felt and lived experience and are pleased with extraordinary signs that indicate to the group that they are touched by the Spirit, if not renewed. They opt for forms of meditation and mind control, and, for those who need more reassurance, there is a turning to a fundamentalist reading of the bible with fundamentalism's recurring themes of the Second Coming and the concerted lament for *The Late Great Planet Earth.*

The final element of a classic revival is synthesis or restoration. This is the conversion aftermath. People are converted to and committed to the new ways and forms that have emerged, whatever they might be. The real and the ideal are now closer together. The process of settling down to security and order can commence. Conscience has been reassured, fervor has been renewed, religion reasserted in a new mode, the covenant reworded, and practical realities and norms revised. The revival is over. It has done its work—that is, revivals

> restore our cultural verve and our self-confidence, helping us to maintain faith in ourselves, our ideals, and our "covenant" with God even while they compel us to reinterpret that covenant in the light of new experience. . . . [They] constitute the awakening of a people caught in an outmoded, dysfunctional world view to the necessity of converting their mindset, their behavior, and their institutions to more relevant or more functionally useful ways of understanding and coping with the changes in the world they live in.[5]

Remember that we are only looking at the phenomenon of a revival from an analytic point of view. We make no judgment of the genuine spiritual unliftings, the fervent change in people's lives and the full joy of the Lord for them. We just want to segregate the elements so that we can apply them to revivals past and present. As a tool they may, as we said before, help our parish focus.

3

A quick glance at our history shows that there have been four revivals or Great Awakenings, each lasting about thirty-five to forty years. The first one went from 1730 to 1760, the second from 1800 to 1830, the third from 1890 to 1920 and the fourth one from 1960 to possibly 1990 if the pattern holds. Each revival had the same five factors we discussed and we ought to look at them briefly to get a feel for the process.

The first revival came from that distortion which resulted when the original Puritan and Calvinistic ideals began to break down, when the original vision of a homogeneous society of saints dissipated. Several tensions appeared. For one thing other different religious persuasions appeared and fractured religious unity. For another the original voluntary principle began to wane. The children of the elect would not always give public affirmation of their affiliation to the faith. Could such children as adults be counted as church members? Could *their* children be baptized? If they were, it was back to an automatic joining without the inner commitment; if they were not they might join up with one of the proliferating sects. So the dilemma was before them: "To allow the children of saints to be counted as full church members without their own acceptable professions of regeneration was to dilute church membership, but not to allow them the right to have their children baptized was to deepen dissatisfaction with the whole system and to narrow its base of support."[6] Family life was under further tension when, land being scarce, sons moved westward carrying with them few possessions and much guilt (remember they were raised in obedience to their fathers and the Father in heaven; leaving was not comfortable). The witchcraft trials in Salem in 1692 reflected difficulties, and with economic expansion the people were confronted with a distinct shift in interest to marketplace realities instead of things of the spirit.

Social inequities grew:

> ... There was a widening gap between the wealthier, aristocratic groups gathered largely in the seaboard centers in places of political and economic power, and the poorer orders of society.... The newly-arrived Germans and Scotch-Irish normally found themselves in such limited circumstances; many were shunted to the hinterland where the struggle for existence was both difficult and dangerous. At the bottom of the social structure were the indentured servants, who could hope to rise when their term was over, and the Negro slaves, who could not. Their social difference showed themselves in church life: in New England where seating in the meeting-house was by rank, in Virginia by the self-perpetuation of the vestries by the uppermiddle classes after 1660.... In New England the percentage of support for church life was apparently relatively high, but in the middle and southern colonies a majority seems to have been effectively out of touch with church life.... The breakdown of familiar patterns in European Christendom constituted a threat in the eyes of the majority of Christians. The structure for maintaining common patterns of morality and values seemed to be decaying. To many of the devout in both

> establishment and dissenting congregations, spiritual lethargy and indifference appeared to be undermining the Christian destiny of the New World in which there had been such high hopes.[7]

Add to this the lure of profit, the burden of the old trade restrictions, the new capitalism waiting to be born, and an Industrial Revolution from England in the wings and you can see the sources of distortion, confusion, and guilt.

The first Great Awakening or revival took place in this context. Major figures were Jonathan Edwards in New England, Gilbert Tennet in the middle colonies, and Samuel Davis in the south. The revival occurred in these areas, although not with equal timing or intensity and it certainly did not include everyone. It was controversial from the beginning, and there was an undercurrent of opposition even during the first preaching tour of the spell-binding George Whitefield, an associate of John Wesley, when he was carrying all before him. The message was one of repentance and love. God forgave the people their sinful ways, and if they repented all could be saved—a radical departure from the predestination of Calvinism, be it noted. With messages like this, given with great oratory and persuasiveness in large meetings, it was no wonder that joy and relief flowed into the stern, guilt-ridden citizen. No wonder they cried, fainted, converted, rejoiced, and witnessed at the massive revival meetings. They were truly "born again," experiencing inner conversions. The poor and disenfranchised especially took to the revivals in great numbers.

The first Great Awakening released guilt, legitimatized the new commerce and trade, blessed the new family relationships and freedoms, and renewed the religious soul of the nation. It even rerouted the notion of the millennium.

Formerly it was thought that Christ would come first and then the millennium would follow. Now it was said that the millennium would be before the coming. The suspicion was thereby aroused that America might possibly have started that millennium or shortly would; it was a new paradise, and a model for the rest of the world. And note that the participation of lay men and women in the revivals showed that religion was democratized as well as politics. All the world could see that it was not rank or status or education that entitled one to witness, but one's religious experience and conversion. And the revivals did much more for the nation than save individual souls:

> The Great Awakenings were primarily religious movements, concerned with bringing sinners to conviction of sin into a dependence on the God who alone could save. They nevertheless had important political as well as social and educational consequences. The intercolonial character of the movement, with its patterns of itineracy as evangelists moved from colony to colony, did much to spread common interests and loyalties among a people who had been largely isolated from one another. Many of the bonds of national feeling that later helped to give a sense of unity to a people were forged in the warmth of religious revival. . . . The Awakenings did stress individual morality, but they also offered visions of a people under God dedicated to the right. . . . The millennial affirmations that were so often a part of the revivals declared that the dreams would become realities in God's good time—which might not be long deferred . . . instilling into American souls a sense of special destiny for the New World nation.[8]

Again, we see the forging of America as the nation with the soul of a church.

The second Great Awakening or revival (1800–1830)

came from the cultural and religious distortions of the postrevolutionary period. The war had brought destruction and had scattered many of the congregations. Interest was transferred from religion to political questions—and something more. This was the era of rationalism and deism, the God of Reason as deduced from the multiplying scientific discoveries that were being made at this time. Through the laws of science, man could change this world and be in charge of his own destiny. Such were the promises of natural religion. Skepticism grew. Challenges to the conventional view of God arose and, for the first time, publicly, questions about his existence. It was at this time that the first book to openly attack Christianity, *Reason the Only Oracle of Man* by Ethan Allen (yes, the hero of Ticonderoga transmuted into a latter-day furniture salesman) appeared (1784), followed ten years later by Thomas Paine's *The Age of Reason.* Besides, it was a time of optimism—hadn't they won the Revolutionary War? There was little need or taste for a religion that reminded man of his lowly, sinful status. So, according to the new deism, man could carve out his own destiny; according to the old religion, his fate was in the hands of an inscrutable, not a "reasonable" God. Distortion was growing all along the line.

The leaders and charismatic figures of this revival were men like Timothy Dwight, grandson of Jonathan Edwards, Lyman Beecher, Moses Stuart, Nathanial William Taylor, James McCready, and the most famous, Charles Finney. Their message was the sinfulness of man, of course, but a sinfulness that could be overcome. A man can, in the twinkling of an eye, in a moment of grace-filled conversion, be truly changed. Then they went on to something more startling: so can a whole nation in like manner. The implication was that the old traditions and customs are not forever valid and binding. Society, like individuals, can change and work in harmony with God's will. Human exertion in partnership with the Holy Spirit was the unbeatable combination. (Note the long road from predestination to the therapeutic blessing of newness and change and the consequent relief of guilt.) Here too were many conversions and dramatic changes and a turning inward which found its fullest expression in the "inner light" of the Quakers. This inner looking was at least safe, because the revivals in general were not apt to take on social issues. At this time it was felt wrong to tamper with these issues, especially sensitive matters like slavery. In time the revival petered out, as it must, stumbling both over the slavery issue and certain untimely predictions for the second coming of Christ. A William Miller, for example, announced that coming for the precise date of October 22, 1844. When the coming did not materialize disillusionment followed and helped extinguish the impact of the second revival. But the impulse, of course, did not die and found its next expression in the third national revival.

The third revival of 1890 to 1920 was the result of those major modern revelations of Darwinism and Freudianism. Darwin came along and challenged the old biblical view of a fixed segregated system of creation. He challenged the whole foundation of the moral law by his theory of the survival of the fittest. Freud was taking away free will with his talk about the subconscious. And while scholars were showing the bible to be filled with contradictions geologists were saying that the earth was much, much older than the bible allowed. Man himself was being reduced to a subspecies which might disappear like any other. If there was a God, he did not seem to be needed beyond some vague job as Prime Mover, First Cause, or Vital Energy. There was incredible distortion growing up between the old biblical view and the new scientific theses. Politically and socially immigrants, mostly Catholic, were making an impact on the country, raising Protestant fears of a take-over. Racism, discrimination, unemployment, rampant capitalism, and a global war were additional stress and anxiety factors. On all fronts, therefore, realities and vision were very far apart.

Some revivalists took a distinctly reactionary stance in view of the threats of Darwin and Freud. They lapsed into Protestant fundamentalism. There was talk once more of an imminent second coming and once more, a turn to introspection as people went back to the bible and discovered the charism of speaking in tongues in the early church. The social order remained unexamined. Dwight Moody offered the work ethic to overcome unemployment. He exhorted his revivalist audience to look to their personal relationship with God. If this was brought into harmony then the blessing of prosperity would follow. Henry Ward Beecher simply said that poverty was the result of sin. The most popular of them all, Billy Sunday, castigated "Demon Rum" as the chief cause of life's ills, an issue which culminated in the Protestant crusade that got prohibition passed in 1920 and repealed thirteen years later. The emergence of noon prayer meetings in New York met with great popularity under strong lay leadership and the wide coverage of the press.

Other revivalists transmuted the faith into Liberal Protestantism which had become embarrassed by the miraculous and so reworked the biblical data by saying such things as "evolution is God's way of doing things." Their optimistic catchwords to help America get on course again were rationalism, efficiency, and, above all, education. These would solve all problems and usher in the millennium. Some did move out into social questions at this time and the Social Gospelers, as they were called, worked closely with Theodore Roosevelt and Woodrow Wilson to bring about "square deals" and "new freedoms." But fundamentally or liberally there was at the turn of the century much distortion that needed the therapies and syntheses of the religious revival.

There is a fourth revival going on now, and this we will examine in the next chapter. For the moment, however, we set aside all of the history and details and simply try to get a feel that there's a long tradition at work here in this "God- obsessed" nation. No matter what the provocation, the nation reverts to seeking faith answers to national and personal dilemmas. Moreover there are measurable elements that lead up to a revival and elements that work it through to a new synthesis. Our examination is asking: Can such history, can such elements give us clues as to what we are going through today and how to assess our own revival?

Notes for Chapter 2

1. *Democracy in America,* trans. Henry Reeve, rev. ed. Fr. Francis Bowen and Philip Bradley (Alfred A. Knopf, 1953), p. 303.

2. Garry Wills, "What Religious Revival?" *Psychology Today* (April 1978), p. 80. Wills adds a further interesting remark, namely, "a datum that certain professors find embarrassing. You could leave Henry Steele Commager's *Empire of Reason* (1977) with the impression that religion had nothing to do with our national origins." This is a deserved rebuke against certain professional antireligious prejudices among intellectuals.

3. Quoted in Claude Gerest, "The Hour of Charisms: The Development of the Charismatic Movements in America," *Concilium* 109 (Seabury Press, 1978), p. 16.

4. William G. McLoughlin, *Revivals, Awakenings, and Reform* (University of Chicago Press, 1978), p. 12. I have relied on this

book and Jay Dolan's *Catholic Revivalism: The American Experience* (University of Notre Dame Press, 1978) for general insights of this and the next chapter.

5. McLoughlin, *Revivals, Awakenings, and Reform,* pp. 2, 8. See also Timothy P. Weber, *Living in the Shadow of the Second Coming* (Oxford University Press, 1979).

6. Robert T. Handy, *A History of the Churches in the United States and Canada* (Oxford University Press, 1977). See also Sydney Ahlstrom's large and detailed *A Religious History of the American People* (Yale University Press, 1972).

7. Handy, *History of Churches,* pp. 73–75.

8. Ibid., p. 114.

3. The Catholic Revival

1

Before we look into the current fourth American revival we should go back and see what the Catholics were doing all this time. They were doing the same thing as the Protestants: they were holding periodic revivals. They simply started later for the simple reason that in the beginning of the nations' history there were not many Catholics around. In the late 1700s and early 1800s Catholics were a tiny minority. They had few churches and fewer clergy. Perhaps this was just as well for it gave the American Catholic church time to organize and plant roots, and it gave time for the revival movement in Europe to iron out the wrinkles before being imported to the new nation.

The Catholic revival was the same as the Protestant revival. It just went under a different name. It was called the mission. This mission/revival went back to post-Reformation times in Europe and was led by the religious orders, especially the newly founded Jesuits. The parish mission spread to Italy and France under the new order of Vincentians and to Germany under the Redemptorists who, in the eighteenth century, brought it to its peak of popularity. After the eighteenth century the mission/revival in Europe declined for a while. Certain exaggerations had sprung up, the novelty had worn off, the Jesuits had been suppressed, and the church in general was under suspicion for its close political ties, often touched upon by the mission. But after the 1820s and the 1840s the mission/revival caught a second breath, just in time to be imported to the New World.

It came with the waves of immigration. As we said, there were few Catholics before the 1800s, but thereafter the numbers grew rapidly. From a population of 318,000 in 1830 the church grew to over one and a half million by 1850 and three million by 1860. These Catholic immigrants, many not speaking English, settled heavily in the northeast, the midwest regions east of the Mississippi and north of the Ohio river. These were the economic centers of the country and the immigrants were by and large a working class people quite low on the rungs of the occupational ladder. Naturally, the number of clergy grew as they too came with the immigrants. During those years they rose from two hundred thirty-two to over two thousand. The number of parish churches grew from two hundred thirty to almost twenty-four hundred. By 1860 forty-three dioceses had been organized, four times that of 1830. To meet the overwhelming challenge of all these people and to help acclimate them to the New World, no less than thirty-five major church councils were held in the United States between 1829 and 1900. And to help bring order, stability, and spiritual renewal to these hordes of people and to give them a sense of belonging, the Catholic mission/revival was just the thing.

By 1829 the mission/revival had become an accepted feature of Catholic evangelization especially after the arrival of the Redemptorists in 1832. It spread like wildfire as more orders joined the circuit: the Passionists took it up in 1856, the newly founded Paulists in 1858, and the Dominicans in 1860. As expected there were differences from the European model. The American mission/revival carried none of the troublesome political overtones as it had in Europe. Although, like the Protestant ones it was highly individualistic, it also had a communal dimension, seeing itself as an aid to forming new parishes, extending old ones and supporting the authority and power of the local pastors. And, unlike the Protestant revivals which appealed mainly to the middle class, the Catholic ones reached out to the lower classes and the marginal Catholic as well. Its appeal lay in its combination of two strains: as befits a highly ritualistic church the Catholic mission/revival displayed with force the traditional rituals and yet, at the same time, it projected pietistic, evangelical elements. So the appeal was wide. That is why many nonaligned citizens were converted and why there was a very high conversion rate among other ritual denominations such as the Episcopalians and Lutherans. Other obvious differences from the Protestant revivals were the promoting of Catholic devotions such as the rosary, the mission cross, the renewal of the baptismal vows, the high point confession, and the opportunity to buy basic instruction books such as Cardinal Gibbons' popular *Faith Of Our Fathers.*

However, the similarities to the Protestant revivals were greater than the differences. The Catholic mission/revival was also born of the rhythms of distortion, confusion, therapy, introspection, and restoration. They too drew large crowds with rousing sermons, dramatic gestures, and startling conversions. The Catholic scene was as moving as any Methodist tent-meeting. One newspaper account in 1848 said that one Redemptorist's sermon "drew tears of repentance and consolation from the eyes of his hearers. Often there was general sobbing and weeping throughout the church".[1] The people were urged to personal conversion and repentance, to immediate and heartfelt experiences of the Lord in their lives—in a word, they were prompted to be "born again." Once again, the head was not as important as the heart. And to help this inner, personal conversion the revivalists would use any device, paint any picture. They would detail the terrible wounds of the crucified Christ, they would carry buckets of blood to the mission cross. They would give morbid descriptions of impending doom and shake people to their boots with descriptions of the unrepentant deathbed scene and the four last things of death, judgment, heaven, and hell. Everything was used to dispose the individual to the awaiting mercy of a forgiving Lord. Sincerity of conversion in the Catholic mission/revival was the general confession at the end, the number of which was always the best indicator of the mission's success.

The speaking style was evangelical, and its echoes are distinctly heard today in the voices of Protestant Oral Roberts or Catholic John Bertolucci. Bodily cures were effected in the blessing of the sick, and extraordinary healings were recorded. One popular missionary wrote that "for nearly forty years cures followed cures without interruption."[2] Millennialism stayed intact, for Catholics too came to see America as the future hope of the church. Isaac Hecker, for example, the Redemptorist missionary who founded the Paulists, said that the "nations' destiny and the interests of God's church are at stake." Finally, like the Protestant counterpart, there was no stress on any social gospel:

> The cultural values fostered at the revival stressed the gospel of acceptance. People were told to be happy with their lot; not to be embarrassed by the absence of power, wealth, and

honor. . . . To have an "itch for money" was a sure ticket to hell. In this manner, revival religion not only rendered the inequality of the social system meaningful by explaining how the poor would inherit the earth, but also shaped the social order of the Catholic subculture by instilling in people a gospel of acceptance.[3]

The Catholic revivalist scene, in short, was cut very much from the same cloth as the Protestant one.

2

Having seen the roots of revivalism, both Protestant and Catholic, let us now take a look at the current revival and how we, as a church, are working through it. All of the five elements are present, as a little reflection will show. It is obvious, for example, that distortion and confusion abound. There is a great deal of tension still between the old and the new. The old consensus has broken down; the norms and blueprints of a former way of life no longer match daily experience. The scientific optimism of a previous age has given way to general pessimism as we ponder nuclear waste disposal problems, radiation levels, persistent war, poverty, juvenile delinquency, crime in the streets, family break-ups, shortages, and economic recessions. People feel out of control of their lives as sociologists, psychologists, mass media programmers, and assorted experts take over.[4] With the growing possibility of a global nuclear accident, untold genetic defects, falling skylabs, and the unleasing of powers science cannot control people are once more "off center." The lying and deceit of some government officials, general cheating in business, the squeeze of oil cartels, shortages of commodities, the world's highest divorce rate, new lifestyles proliferating daily—all have shaken people's confidence. A dislocated generation caught in cultural distortion (future shock) is aptly described as living in the Age of Anxiety or being a part of the Lonely Crowd. Religion, traditionally the interpretative bedrock of stability is caught up in the same cultural shifts:

> The old priests, pastors, and rabbis simply could not provide answers to the most pressing problems, let alone to national and world problems; the younger priests, pastors, and rabbis seemed as rebellious and divided as their flocks. Authorities within the church pitted the faithful against each other; and, if anyone turned outside the church, to the scientists, the answers were equally contradictory. Birth control and population control constituted only one such unanswerable question. Women's liberation and the use of abortion were even more controversial. There seemed to be no clear religious or scientific guidelines for old or young. The churches did not know whether homosexuals (let alone transexuals) could be "orthodox" or have congregations to meet their needs. Neither scientists nor ministers could agree on whether a fetus was human (or *when* it was), whether Karen Quinlan was a vegetable, whether euthanasia was more merciful than prolonged cancer. Ordinary people were left without guidance or consolation on the most pressing of all questions—on love, life, and death.[5]

In such uncertainties, as might be expected, therapies and therapists abound. Billy Graham is to this generation, for example, what Billy Sunday was to his.[6] Institutional religion, to no one's surprise, is a bad word. Inner experience is "in" once again. The popular press continue to headline the phenomena by speaking of a new revival in religion. We now know that they are wrong. There is no "revival," there is only a continuation of the old rhythms planted within the foundation of our country. Once again Garry Wills is on the mark when he writes, "The roots of American religiosity are deep and tangled. . . . They reveal an American religious ethos that survives still. There are, of course, changes in the manifestations of American piety, shifts and surface developments; but they are less important than the larger steadiness and energy of the religious instinct among us. American religion is, even now, not a marvel of rebirth but of vigorous old age. It is not Lazarus, but Methuselah."[7]

In such current revivalist "distortion" it is expected that attendance at the mainline churches would slip drastically. They have and, as also expected, the "inner-feeling" evangelical churches have grown dramatically. *U.S. News and World Report* indicates, for example, that the United Methodists are down by ten percent, the Episcopalians by fifteen percent, the United Presbyterians by ten percent. On the other hand the Southern Baptists are up by eighteen percent, the Assemblies of God by thirty-seven percent and the Seventh Day Adventists by thirty-four percent.[8] The evangelicals are, of course, no longer tied to the old tent or meeting hall. These days they hire huge auditoriums, go on commercial television, and into highly profitable publishing. The number of religious radio stations has doubled since 1972. Evangelists collectively claim an average weekly radio audience of 115 million and a television weekly audience of 14 million. Both ventures are liberally supported by "born again" Christians. The proceeds from some of the television evangelicals will give an idea of the magnitude of the current revival. Oral Roberts' ministry takes in about 60 million dollars a year; the Church of God, 65 million; the Christian Broadcast Network, 58 million; Billy Graham Evangelistic Crusade, 38 million; Praise the Lord Club, 25 million.[9] Current therapists include Oral Roberts, Billy Graham, Bill Bright, Pat Robertson, Robert Schuller. Born again books are phenomenal bestsellers. They include *Born Again* (Charles Colson), *The Possible Dream* (Charles Paul Conn), *Soul on Fire* (Eldridge Cleaver), *The Hiding Place* (Corrie Ten Boom), and the works of Ruth Carter Stapleton and a host of others.

The thrust, once again, is conservative and a turning inward, a searching for experience. Jews therefore are experiencing direct personal encounters with God in the revival of orthodoxy and in a rising interest in Hasidism, Protestants in Pentecostalism, and Catholics in charismatic movements. We should remember that underlying these pietistic movements in all three faiths is a loss of faith in the old forms, doctrines, and rituals and the feeling that the leaders who used to explain God's will are now incapable of doing so. The same tendency to focus on the inside to the exclusion of the larger social issues also persists—although of late there has been a distinct turnaround in some of the evangelical philosophies.

There is something new, however, in the revival of our global village; that is, the choice of exotic alternatives to the mainline churches. While the evangelical churches are reaping large numbers, world culture has enabled people, especially the young, to turn to alternative lifestyles and to Eastern offerings. The "beat" generation of a while back tried to celebrate the playful side of life and its uncomplicatedness by contemplating a simple flower and emphasizing that heaven is within you. Others, sensing that Western civilization was going bankrupt, turned to the cults. They were disgusted with America's materialism and opted for "intuitive awareness" induced by drugs or expressed in "flower power," Jesus People, Hinduism, Zen,

Taoism, I Ching, and even rock concerts. Some among the young, suffering from America's overchoices and burdened with guilt over their own family lives, attached themselves to the first guru who came along and, in an ironic restoration of the old Calvinism (or, as some would say, in Freudian repentance), gave themselves once more in total obedience and submission to their new "father" who, as in the case of Rev. Moon of the Unification church, may even choose their spouses for them. Whatever we may think of these movements, we must at least appreciate that "the search for another order of reality in these 'outlandish' activities marked the failure of the ordinary religious institutions to provide satisfactory answers about the mysterious, the unknown, the unexplainable, and, of course, it also marked the failure of science to do so."[10]

3

It is time to see the reactions some of our Catholic people have taken in the current revival. The answers should not surprise us. Catholics, as Americans, have taken the same route in their own way as their Protestant associates, and often, through ecumenism, have melded their efforts. The dynamics are the same, the five elements are the same. The cursillo movement was among the first to give people a more personal expression, commitment, and security in a distorting world. The liturgical movement was meant to do the same, although it went the way of the head instead of the heart and so has floundered. Then came the marriage encounter, bible studies, prayer groups, and, most of all, the largest and most appealing of them all, the charismatic movement. Significantly it started on a college campus for, as Peter Berger points out, it is largely an upper middle class movement reflecting a need for people searching for more certain identity in an official church that grew less and less sure of its own. But these movements and many others are tapping the old roots: they are expressions of the persistent pietistic side of the old structured, ritualistic religion. "Catholicism was and still is a very ritually orientated religion, but at certain moments in its history the spirit of evangelicalism complemented and even overshadowed the piety of ritual. This experiential strain of religion has always been present in Catholic piety. Francis of Assisi underscored the importance of experiential religion, as did Teresa of Avila, Ignatius of Loyola, and Alphonsus de Liguori. They called people to reform and repent, and all of them emphasized the importance of personal conversion. In time the fires of enthusiasm would cool off, and the evangelical piety would once again be overshadowed by the religion of ritual until that moment when the spirit of renewal rekindled the need for call to conversion and repentance."[11]

There is no doubt, then, that the charismatic movement is yet another creative pietistic strain that has periodically emerged in Catholicism, yet another revival in the tradition of all the others. That is why the literal answer to the book *A New Pentecost?* by the movement's chief official supporter, Cardinal Suenens is, "No, of course not. It is the old Pentecost." Its immediate roots go back to the nineteenth century "holiness" movements which were abetted by the Second Great Awakening and other revivals. The holiness people found that their fellow Protestants were still too much with the world. They were even more appalled by those liberal Protestants who seemed to launder the bible of any supernatural meaning. They ultimately gave up any hope that any of the standard churches could ever be reformed from within. So they started a kind of separate fellowship of the sanctified. They went into free prayer, bible schooling; they forbade alcohol, entertainment, and sometimes tobacco. They were immensely emotional and their meetings were filled with visions, healings, and the speaking in tongues which became common after 1886, years before the Pentecostal Movement was founded.

It was from this kind of people that Pentecostalism arose. It began in Topeka, Kansas in 1900 from a group of people, mostly of the holiness tradition, who wondered why they did not receive that baptism of the Spirit so evident in the New Testament and which resulted in the speaking in tongues. They prayed over this and in 1901 such speaking in tongues did occur. Thus was born Pentecostalism with its strong tongue-speaking association, the most obvious sign that the Spirit was at work. We should remember, however, that some holiness people, decades before, had spoken in tongues and other sects such as the Mormons and the Irvingites had tongue speaking. They just did not make it their chief characteristic. A Pastor Charles Parham spread the new movement and a black Baptist, William Seymour, in the Azusa Mission in Los Angeles gave it a further boost by joining the speaking in tongues with the baptism of the Spirit. Pentecostalism became particularly strong among the Puerto Ricans and the blacks, and there was no doubt that it provided at the time for many misfits in an industrial society a channel through which they could express their bewilderment and at the same time discover some kind of spiritual home. It sought truth in lived experience, not in doctrine; it sought to find immediate verification in the moral life of the community and to not accept God unless one could do so with the whole of oneself.

True to its fundamentalist mentality the Pentecostal

movement proclaimed millennialist ideas. Its very first paper from the Azusa Mission stated that "many are the prophecies spoken in unknown tongues and many the visions that God is giving concerning His soon coming".[12] It is interesting how persistent this millennialist inclination has remained right up to the present time. Many have tried to analyze it and some have attempted to give reasons for the fascination of the immediate second coming. First of all, the bible itself clearly teaches a second coming even though it gives no date.[13] Secondly, millennialism for some is a hedge against death. If you are among the elect you will not have to die but, as St. Paul says, you will be "caught up in the air" or "raptured" before the horrible end descends on the others.[14] Thirdly, there is what some call the "psychology of deliverance"; that is, all the problems and all the crises of one's life will finally be eliminated by the appearance of the Lord, so his quick coming is something dearly to desire and long for. Fourthly, for many conservative people it stands as a rebuke to the liberal erosion of doctrine. "For many evangelicals today, the premillennial second coming, the divinity of Jesus, the virgin birth, the resurrection, the substitutionary atonement, and the infallibility of the bible come as a self-contained doctrinal package, allowing no addition or subtractions."[15] Finally, according to the devotees, everything pointing to the second coming seems verified; all the signs, the hints, the necessary portents are there: catastrophes, wars, famine, and, most of all, the required "return of the Jews" in the founding of the state of Israel in 1948. There is no doubt that the end is forever near.

After the speaking in tongues and belief in the proximate second coming, the last characteristic of the Pentecostal and evangelical tradition is healing and the casting out of demons. There is obviously a connection for people who are at home in the spirit world. To speak in tongues and to deal in healing are involvements of spirit. In healing and tongue speaking, however, the Holy Spirit is the agent. In sickness, evil spirits are at work. Healings become a process of driving out the evil spirits through the greater power of the Holy Spirit.

We have taken time to mention these characteristics because the modern reader will readily recognize the very same ones in vogue today and, as one author says, "to have endured so long, to be continually revived in new forms like Pentecostalism, to thrive even in the centers of modern culture, ecstatic religion must satisfy human needs that are widespread indeed." [16] The modern parish will have to take into account what those human needs are and perhaps learn how to integrate such notions into its scope.

But let us move on. The rhythms of the old Pentecostal movement emerged in time onto what is called neo-Pentecostalism or the charismatic movement. It began to catch hold in the respectable mainline churches around the 1960s with the Lutherans and Episcopalians. Then it started up in the Catholic church in 1966 among students at Duquesne University in Pittsburgh. From there it moved to Notre Dame when several in a group there received the gift of baptism in the Spirit. After 1970 the movement spread rapidly among Catholics. For the most part, however, the Catholic experience has been somewhat different (and here we see the influence of the old mission/revival): Catholic charismatics have been quite ready to integrate the movement into the church and not to draw apart from it. Since there is really no new doctrine attached to the charismatic movement they found that they could keep their old credo and that the baptism of the Spirit does not interfere with the sacraments of baptism and confirmation. Rather, as one of their chief spokesmen,

Kevin Ranaghan, puts it, "it comes as an adult reaffirmation and renewal of these sacraments, an opening of ourselves to all the graces they bring." Another early apologist says, "It is true that in the Catholic Church the mood of Pentecostalism has altered noticeably: it has become more quiet and gentle, less demonstrative. Nevertheless, the experience of the 'baptism in the Spirit' and the appearance of charisms leave no doubt that it is the same Spirit that is at work here as elsewhere. On the other hand, the Catholics who have accepted Pentecostal spirituality have found it to be fully in harmony with their traditional faith and life. They experience it, not as a borrowing from an alien religion, but as a connatural development of their own."[17]

Basically, however, both Protestant and Catholic charismatic movements are present-day versions of the early revival therapies. Surface differences exist in the Catholic camp in relation to the old Catholic mission/revival: the old revivalist symbols focused on the cross, a good confession, and parish orientation. The charismatic revival focuses on the Holy Spirit, the charisms it bestows, and has the freedom to opt for prayer groups and covenant communities beyond or within the parish structure. But the similarities are striking. Both old and new revivalisms focus very much on personal experience and conversion. To be "born again," to have experience of the Lord, while not demanded are much sought after. Theirs is a religion of the heart. They have their therapists and some excellent theologians, but the popular stance is to feel God's love in your bones. In spite of the efforts and insistence of the leaders a certain antiintellectualism exists as such inner experiences are prized over intellectual understanding. The gift of speaking in tongues, for example, would be much preferred by many to insight.

Emotionalism, as might be expected in any revival, runs high. In the old days it was tearful expressions of sorrow and repenting outbursts beneath the mission cross. These days it tends also to include a more joyful spirit with shouts of "Praise the Lord" beneath a colorful banner. Joining in group prayer is more apt to be preferred to the one-to-one good confession in the box. And the large therapeutic gatherings are as necessary as ever as anyone can testify who has been at the stadiums of the annual Jesus gatherings at which the Catholic orators are as folksy, witnessing evangelicals as Billy Sunday ever was. Like the piety of old, the turning inward has precluded concern for social involvement, an emphasis the current leadership is decidedly trying to turn about. Finally, in the old tradition, there is a keen interest in healing and scores of books testify to the popularity of the subject. Healing, as we have seen, was very much a part of the old mission/revival only then it was associated with sacramental activity; now, for the charismatics, it is wont to be interpreted as the direct outpouring of the Holy Spirit, and there is a real interest in demonology and deliverance.

To the degree that the charismatic movement is kin to the old revivals, it is a counterculture movement. It is a movement that is trying to discover a spirituality for our times, and it may in fact provide us with an understanding and a language for what our churches cannot yet define in our current distortion: new concepts of faith understood by contemporary people. The charismatic movement is offering notions, language, and experience about the essentials of the faith, about Jesus and his gospel. It is offering to bewildered people a sense of identity and inner resources. As Claude Gerest says, people can now "see themselves as dynamic rather then protesting. The revivalists of the camp meeting told us that they reflected the situation of the frontier with its possibilities for expansion. Something of this reflection has remained, although Pentecostalism has left the frontier. The church that is now there to be built up is the church of *aggiornamento* and *oikoumene;* the Spirit invoked, there is, in God, not cold immateriality but the breath of life, he who 'hastens the time,' who pushed back the limits of the possible and shares his joy."[18] There are flaws, misgivings and simplicities,[19] but these should not blind us to God-given therapies that the charismatics and other current movements are giving the church, hastening it to the day of restoration.

Notes for Chapter 3

1. Jay P. Dolan, *Catholic Revivalism* (University of Notre Dame Press, 1978), p. 21.
2. Ibid. p. 146.
3. Ibid. pp. 159, 160.
4. A good insight into the influence of the media is found in David Halberstam, *The Powers That Be* (Alfred A. Knopf, 1979).
5. William G. McLoughlin, *Revivals, Awakenings, and Religion* (University of Chicago Press, 1978), p. 192.
6. For an interesting biography of Graham, see Marshall Frady, *Billy Graham: A Parable of American Righteousness* (Little Brown, 1979). For his change of heart on social issues (namely nuclear arms) see *Sojourners* (August 1979).
7. Garry Wills, *Psychology Today* (April 1978) p. 81.
8. *U.S. News and World Report* (October 18, 1978).
9. *The Saturday Review* (February 3, 1979).
10. McLoughlin, *Revivals, Awakenings, and Religion,* p. 208. See also Robert S. Ellwood *Alternative Altars: Unconventional and Eastern Spirituality in America* (University of Chicago Press, 1979). On religious cults and young people see Joel MacCollam, *Carnival of Souls* (Seabury Press, 1979). See also John Garvey, ed., *All Our Sons and Daughters* (Templegate, 1977).
11. Dolan, *Catholic Revivalism,* p. 186.

12. Quoted in Robert Mapes Anderson, *Vision of the Disinherited* (Oxford University Press, 1979), p. 79.

13. An Archbishop Ussher who died in 1656 estimated that mankind had 6000 years to exist and therefore from his biblical calculations the world should end somewhere between 1896 and 1901. Then the millennium would commence.

14. An author who says that Jesus' own words refutes such doomsdayers is Robert Jewett, *Jesus Against the Rapture* (Westminster Press, 1979). See also Carl A. Raschke, "Eschatology As The Revelation of the Interpersonal" *Cross Currents* (Spring 1979).

15. Timothy P. Weber, *Living in the Shadow of the Second Coming* (Oxford University Press, 1979), p. 179. For a fine critique of other current works on the millennium see Leonard I. Sweet, "Millennialism in America," *Theological Studies* 40, No. 3 (September 1979), p. 510ff.

16. Anderson, *Vision of the Disinherited,* p. 8. Anyone interested in the tongues phenomenon might consult William J. Samarin, *Tongues of Men and Angels* (Macmillan, 1972), and Anderson's book mentioned here and note his observation: "There were some Pentecostals in America who conceded that speaking in tongues was sometimes unintelligible, and many Europeans who acknowledged it was usually so, yet they continued to speak in tongues and to believe it was the work of the Spirit. For what was important to the tongue-speaker was not the actual sounds themselves—that became a problem only for the dogmatic apologists of the movement—but rather the sense of possessing and being possessed by the Holy Spirit" (p. 92).

17. Edward D. O'Connor, C.S.C., *The Pentecostal Movement in the Catholic Church* (Ave Maria Press, 1971), p. 28. See also David Edwin Harrell, *All Things Are Possible: The Healing and Charismatic Revivals in America* (Indiana University Press, 1979).

18. Claude Gerest, "The Hour of Charisms: The Development of the Charismatic Movements in America," *Concilium* 109 (Seabury Press, 1978), p. 35.

19. See John Koenig, *Charismata: God's Gifts for God's People* (Westminster Press, 1978). See also Simon Tugwell et al., *New Heaven? New Earth?* (Templegate, 1976).

4. The Sojourners

1

Practical applications beg to be made from all that we have so far seen. Before we do that, however, let us briefly round out the picture with a little history of the parish structure and one contemporary description of it. We begin with priest-sociologist Andrew Greeley's observation that "institutional Catholicism in the United States prospered as long as it did because it provided self-definition and social location for the immigrants, their children, and their grandchildren; and it did so precisely through the institution of the neighborhood parish."[1] Although the neighborhood has changed a great deal these days, and whole sections have decayed or prospered and changed complexion, and there is much mobility and the crossing of parish lines in search of a satisfying liturgy or sermon, the concrete parish complex in an area is still effective, or can be—and that is the conviction of this book. Movements come and go, subgroups flourish here and there, gifted individuals or communes crop up to challenge us with basic gospel, but still, as the early church learned, there is need for a center of stability and order. There still seems to be a need for a larger, overall gathering of mixed people united in a common faith visibly linked to the bishop and to the universal church. Movements and sub-groups are by definition homogenous. As such they represent only one aspect of what community is meant to be. But the parish also by definition is a catch-all assembly, cutting across liberal-conservative lines, status and age, a wide embrace of rooted tradition. In one form or another it will be here for a long time. That is why I was so captivated with the announcement of the Taize Weekend of Hope made by two of its community Brothers. It read:

> On June 22 and 23 St. Patrick's Church in Bayshore will welcome to a weekend of hope all people who are seeking the new face of the church as a place of communion for all. Over the past few years people have begun to form groups in order to bridge the gap between faith and life, to struggle for justice, and to uncover the very sources of the spiritual life. This has happened within the churches, but increasingly people have tended to gather and to struggle apart from the traditional parish. We are challenged to heal this separation, because the parish is not merely a copy of a human organization; it is, in miniature, that unique communion called the church, from which no one is excluded. We are challenged to participate in the creation of a Christian community which can truly become the community of communities. In this community those who work now outside of the churches will find paths to reconciliation; in turn, the parishes will be transfigured by many new visions.

This is why, at long last, it is so comforting to see that our ecclesiastical leaders are belatedly coming to conclusions that we in the field have known all along: the parish is durable, important, flexible, critical, and here to stay. No other structure offers quite so much to so many. The leaders are suddenly realizing that and, along with evangelization and the family, have made parish renewal their top priority of concern. They, the bishops, have shown a whole new interest in this basic ward unity of the church politic. Our church leaders, themselves too long absent from parish life, are realizing that, for better or for worse, the large majority of Catholics at critical times of their lives will touch base with a local parish, not the Church Universal. They will enter into the mysterious rhythms of birth, marriage, sickness, and death vis à vis the parish. The impression that the parish-community makes at these archetypal times will be lasting and often will be a critical factor in the subconscious appreciation of the church's mission. For all so involved, Catholic and non-Catholic, the parish will form a lasting impression of what they think "the church" is all about.

The Catholic church in all of its history, aspirations, and pretensions is relayed through the parish for the average citizen. There is no doubt that, as a kind of summary of the whole Catholic experience, the local parish gives off many stimuli which attract, repel, and color people's feel for religion in general and for the church in particular. It is like what Dr. Peck says about children in his book *The Road Less Travelled,* "It is not so much what our parents say that determines our worldview as it is the unique world they create for us by their behavior."[2] So with the parish. It creates a worldview by its behavior, by what it does, what it signifies. In many ways, it is the first ecclesiastical hand that rocks the organized religious cradle. It should not be treated lightly and every bishop should be persuaded, cajoled, and even threatened to send his best men and women into the front line. The unspoken system has been for too long to reward the most "talented" and the most "respectable" people with remote chancery or department jobs leaving the distinct impression that any old warm body can shepherd a parish. The current reward of monsignor has been made bankrupt and suspect by tilting so heavily in favor of office-bound men and administrators as to show prejudice against those in the pastoral field. From my biased view I have always thought that those in "special ministries" should be shorn of such pretensions and be dubbed as being in "assisting ministries"; that is, assisting the parish. For the simple arithmetic is that before any human being gets to meet his or her chaplain, campus minister, retreat master, or tribunal official that individual first has had to pass through the influence of the local parish community. And this includes even bishops who once were little boys making their first holy communion. Perhaps there would be less need of therapeutic officials, bureaus, and evangelization programs if the front line had been gracious in the Lord by having warmly pastoral people give the church's first embrace.

We should also realize the enormous importance the parish plays, or could play, in the mutual enrichment and believability of the "two churches"; for, as William McCready reminds us, we are really operating two distinct churches: the official one with its rules and bureaucracy (not meant pejoratively) and the popular church of everyday life. There is the official church with its tradition and the daily local parish church of the street and the neighborhood where life is actually lived. It is when these two churches intersect that there is the possibility of what David Tracy calls "revisionist theology." By that he means when the real-life situations of the everyday scene encounter the conventional tradition of the official church a fruitful exchange and enrichment can take place and a genuine revision emerge. Alienation occurs when these two do not intersect. When this happens people are then forced to part with the official church, even when they have no intention of parting with religion. The moral is that the parish surely needs the tradition of this official church, but it becomes more evident every day in the lengthening list of the dissatisfied that the official church, if it is to reclaim its credibility, needs to intersect with the popular church embodied in the parish.

Finally, the nearly 18,600 parishes in the United States have the potential to do what no other unit can: provide a sense of community for the families of a highly mobile and diverse society. We are hearing now and will be hearing more about families as the bishops' "Year of the Family," which began in 1980, continues to develop for the rest of the decade. ("Family" here has a much broader meaning than just the biological members of a household.) Families, as we all know, are under constant threat and attack by the mass culture. Parents are bewildered as to what to do and how to raise their children with Christian values in a mass media world which subtly and overtly undermines them every day. The individual nuclear family feels not only threatened and powerless but isolated. This sense of isolation came across very strongly in the 800,000 responses to the 1976 "Call to Action" survey. The old extended family is gone, left behind in the latest change of address. Neighborhoods and neighbors are temporary. Married children live far away or are some of the growing divorce statistics. The only thing that is constant is the all pervasive television selling attitudes and lifestyles the parents could do without. Is there anywhere the family can come together where faith can be shared and values affirmed? Some join small prayer groups, the Christian Family Movement, the family cluster movement, marriage encounter, family weekend experiences, but many don't. It falls to the parish, the one stable unit, the one sacramental sign of the compassionate and comforting Christ, to build community for these "pilgrims" of a mobile society. The family may be the "domestic church," to use the phrase of Vatican II, but it needs a home. It needs a larger community of support to survive. The parish is in a unique position to provide this. This fact alone should urge a strong sense of respect for the parish and call forth every kind of aid, support, and encouragement from our leaders.

With this said, we should now, for the sake of completeness, take a look into the origins of the parish, how it got started and how we arrived at the present structure. Intriguingly, we discover that the very word parish has appealing human and biblical overtones. In the Jewish Scriptures (Old Testament) the Hebrew word for parish literally means "sojourners." It means a people visiting a land or traveling through; strangers, not natives. The Israelites were thus "parishioners" or sojourners in their stay in Egypt. We, too, in the Christian scriptures are told that "we have not here a lasting city." This is not our forever home. This ought not to imply, as it has unfortunately done at different times, that we are so committed to our "true" home in heaven that we may safely ignore this incarnational earth. The term is rather meant to give us a fundamental reminder of our global status and personal stance. As Monica Furlong says, "the religious person is the one who believes that life is about making some kind of journey; the nonreligious person is the one who believes that there is no journey to take."[3] So we are religious sojourners, parishioners on our way.

The early communities in the New Testament quickly adapted the term parishioner or sojourner to denote their true citizenship in heaven, but after the year 150 the word became a kind of official term denoting the various communities of Christians in a given place with the bishop at the head. We note that the word parish here really means what we would call a diocese for at that time there were not as yet smaller subdivisions, only large communities in a given area such as Rome or Antioch. The bishop as head had the help of his priests. When the church membership multiplied the bishop allowed his priests to celebrate the eucharist in the outlying districts, but afterwards they returned to his residence for they were but his extensions. One precious sign of the bishops's connection with the smaller districts was his practice of breaking off a piece of the eucharistic bread at his mass and sending it to the other church communities in the city as a sign of unity. This practice continued for several centuries, and we still have a relic of it when, right before communion, the celebrant breaks off a piece of the Holy Bread and drops it into the chalice.

It was not until the fourth century, after the time of Constantine, when the church was eventually made the legal religion of the empire, that the parish came to mean pretty much what we mean by it today. And, as the church pushed even more insistently into the rural areas while the bishops remained in the large cities, the parish found its final shape in its smaller community guided by the priest/pastor. Still, it was considered a subgroup to the larger community (diocese) presided over by the bishop. By the fifth century parishes were acquiring boundaries. After that, when the Middle Ages dawned and feudalism became the norm of society's structure, the parish went into a very checkered career. This was because local lords, dukes, counts, petty kings, and emperors took over much of the land—and the land in which such parishes stood. Being landlords they hired and fired their own clergy who understandably became their vassals. This was hardly satisfactory, but the bishops were helpless. Some bishops tried to make inroads by building parish churches on their own property and seeing to it that baptisms and Mass obligations could only be fulfilled there. But in the eighth century the emperor took over even these so that parish churches were almost entirely in the hands of the civil powers. This precipitated the famous lay investiture controversies by which such emperors and civil rulers invested the clergy with the insignia of their office.

It was not until the reforms of the sixteenth century Council of Trent that parishes as we know them were fully restored as independent units with determined boundaries under the final say of the local bishop. The parish pastor, as the bishop's delegate, was defined as *the* man in charge, and not even the religious orders, with all of their privileges, were to infringe on his rights and power. (There were no such privileges or rights of the laity to speak of—only obligations—but more of this later.) The parish as formed by Trent has endured as a rather closed system and static unity. As such it accurately reflected the rest of society right up to the turn of the century. Since then, as we have seen, drastic social changes have occurred: immigration, mobility, travel, the rise of the suburb, commercial entertainments, mass media, and a host of other supermarket overchoices. These have provided endless distractions and leisure time and so have moved the parish, once the neighborhood physical, spiritual, and emotional center, to the status of one more competitor for the attention of today's parishioner. The parish in particular, like organized religion in general, has become just one more department of lifestyle along with medicine, business, sports, and entertainment in the pages of *Time* and *Newsweek*. A recent *U.S. News and World Report* survey tells the story. In its poll of "Institutions That Wield the Most Influence" in the world, organized religion ranked twenty-sixth in a field of twenty-nine, far below fifth ranking television, ninth ranking banks, and, unkindest cut of all, sixteenth ranking public opinion polls. Add to this picture the proliferation of many government sponsored social services, once the exclusive arena of the churches, and you can see why the parish is suffering an identity crisis, going through a traditional distortion, and is in need of adjustment.

Furthermore, it is obvious that the model of parish we have been describing above—the one inherited from the Middle Ages, enshrined in canon law and consecrated by the Council of Trent—that this model is the traditional pyramid one. This is the one that emphasized carefully structured and channeled authority, one that simply made the hierarchically layered universal church present on the local level. This model has, of course, been modified by Vatican II. We are working towards a new model, one that might best be described as the "sacramental-communal" model. (We described this in the first chapter and will enlarge on it in later ones). Again, therefore, the local parish, like its larger parent, the universal church, must see itself in a new light. It must begin its painful metamorphosis into a small but powerful sign of God's gracious love in Christ.

2

The whole concept of being parishioners or sojourners brings to mind not only a people headed for a common destiny on a common journey but, most naturally, it hints that such travelers likely tell their stories to each other as they go along. There is every similarity here to a kind of spiritual *Canterbury Tales.* Of late some theologians have picked up the storytelling pilgrimage as one interesting image of the parish (and the church). Such an image has its advantages. For one thing a story, as opposed to a statement, allows for many levels of meaning and experience. Secondly, the story is imprecise, shaded, complex—and so are we. Finally, stories by nature respect and tell of mystery, and you can only live mystery, you cannot dissect it as propositions are apt to do. Stories are like the dances of Martha Graham. She was once asked what one of her dances meant. Quite properly she replied, "Darlings, if I could *tell* you I would not have danced it!" Our common story in faith can likewise only be danced; it lies beyond mere words. Or, to put it another way, stories are more persuasive and powerful than doctrines and have more evangelistic impact. Maybe that's what one black minister meant when he said that while white theologians built logical systems black folk told tales. Maybe that is also what is behind the gentle scolding of the editor of *Parobola* magazine who wrote, "What is needed is what the churches have lost: the kind of knowledge that cannot be put into books, that depends on its transmission on human contact. It cannot emanate from someone who does not have it, nor be received by anyone who thinks he already does. Somewhere, somehow, there are always 'men of knowledge'; but they are recognizable only by the people who know that they do not know, who are open to laughter and to shock, and so are ready to learn."[4]

Stories deal with universal or archetypal themes. We can all identify with discovery, bondage, liberation, surprise, life, death. We can all identify with put-down Cinderellas, set-up simpletons, ugly ducklings, fearful giants, frogs waiting to be released with the accepting kiss. The parish is seen as the local church context that contains and therapeutically acts out these stories. It is a place where in symbol, ritual, and community we openly relate our own personal stories, listen to others tell theirs, and all of us together celebrate them against the larger story which is Christ. We know what it is to feel like the put-down women at Jacob's well, a set-up Peter before courtyard fires, a treed Zacchaeus, and frog Magdalenes. But we also know that our stories are colored with the Good News; namely, that the accepting kiss and the releasing word await us in Jesus. So the parish is the faith-place where most of us live out and share our stories and receive that kiss and word (sacrament and scripture). Here we relate and celebrate our collective stories as we journey together within the two thousand year tradition of millions who have lived out their stories before us. We enshrine in our liturgies the old rondelets of sins committed and forgiven, follies done and forgotten, heroism neglected and rewarded, and death no longer a wall but a window which leads to the land where no more tears are shed. This community storytelling is meaningful because it partakes in Jesus' own story. It is redemptive because Jesus has incarnated himself into our human story so thoroughly that everything human counts: every paragraph, every sentence, every word. And as Risen Lord he has guaranteed our stories the always perfect ending "and they lived happily ever after."

And, as we said, it is a story told in *our* tradition. We Catholics have a peculiar story different from all the others. And it is in this tradition of popes (good and bad), cardinals (conniving and heroic), councils (shallow and profound), laws (patronizing and protective), bishops (arrogant and pastoral), priests (stupid and clever), sacraments (magical and mysterious), and just plain people (sinners and saints, celibates and married, activists and mystics)—it is in *this* tradition that we stand as a parish. Every parish carries the seeds of the peculiarly Roman Catholic shape of the gospel story in which we are formed and in which we shall find salvation. We may wish certain paragraphs deleted from our collective story and others expanded, but we can't do that. We are what we are, a "Christian community in the Roman Catholic tradition" (to quote our own parish motto) and, as the centuries of storytelling have shown, quite able to discover the elements of holiness within its context. And if our stories are told, listened to, acted out and celebrated well locally in the parish, we can perform one of the most needed functions of today: to give meaning to human life. And a meaning that is not by any means a mere repetition of our traditions, a mere retelling, but a meaning derived from our basic roots which nourishes us to dramatic changes, hastens us through our cultural and religious distortions, and organically thrusts us into the unknown restoration ahead.

Perhaps it is fitting that we should close this section with two brief stories that say something about the Christian gospel and our parishes. The first one is from that master, Franz Kafka, called "An Imperial Message":

> The Emperor, so a parable runs, has sent a message to you, the humble subject, the insignificant shadow cowering in the remotest distance before the imperial sun; the Emperor from his deathbed has sent a message to you alone. He has commanded the messenger to kneel down by the bed, and has whispered the message to him; so much store did he lay on it that he ordered the messenger to whisper it back into his ear again. Then by a nod of the head he has confirmed that it is right. Yes, before the assembled spectators of his death—all the obstructing walls have been broken down, and on the spacious and loftily mounting open staircases stand in a ring the great princes of the Empire—before all these he has delivered his message. The messenger immediately sets out on his journey; a powerful, an indefatigable man; now pushing with his right arm, now with his left, he cleaves a way

> for himself through the throng; if he encounters resistance he points to his breast, where the symbol of the sun glitters; the way is made easier for him than it would be for any other man. But the multitudes are so vast; their numbers have no end. If he could reach the open fields how fast he would fly, and soon doubtless you would hear the welcome hammering of his fists on your door. But instead how vainly does he wear out his strength; still he is only making his way through the chambers of the innermost palace; never will he get to the end of them; and if he succeeded in that nothing would be gained; he must next fight his way down the stair; and if he succeeded in that nothing would be gained; the courts would still have to be crossed; and after the courts the second outer palace; and once more stairs and courts; and once more another palace; and so on for thousands of years; and if at last he should burst through the outermost gate—but never, never can that happen—the imperial capital would lie before him, the center of the world, crammed to bursting with its own sediment. Nobody could fight his way through here even with a message from a dead man. But you sit at your window when evening falls and dream it to yourself.[5]

As we resonate with this story the parish, rooted in the apostolic gospel, boldly retells it. In the parish community we hear the Good News, the Better News, that proclaims that in fact the messenger, Jesus, *did* get through with his word from the Emperor (Father) and that therefore we are no longer left to dream and yearn for salvation. And what is the message he brought? It is this: "Your sins, many as they are, are forgiven. The last shall be first. Let us eat and celebrate because this son of mine was dead and has come back to life. He was lost and is found." The parish tells that story in endless ways and versions.

The other story is by Francis Dorff called "The Rabbi's Gift":

There was a famous monastery which had fallen on very hard times. Formerly its many buildings were filled with young monks and its big church resounded with the singing of the chant, but now it was deserted. People no longer came there to be nourished by prayer. A handful of old monks shuffled through the cloisters and praised their God with heavy hearts.

On the edge of the monastery woods, an old rabbi had built a little hut. He would come there from time to time to fast and pray. No one ever spoke with him, but whenever he appeared, the word would be passed from monk to monk: "The rabbi walks in the woods." And, for as long as he was there, the monks would feel sustained by his prayerful presence.

One day the abbot decided to visit the rabbi and to open his heart to him. So, after the morning Eucharist, he set out through the woods. As he approached the hut, the abbot saw the rabbi standing in the doorway, his arms outstretched in welcome. It was as though he had been waiting there for some time. The two embraced like long-lost brothers. Then they stepped back and just stood there, smiling at one another with smiles their faces could hardly contain.

After a while the rabbi motioned the abbot to enter. In the middle of the room was a wooden table with the Scriptures open on it. They sat there for a moment, in the presence of the Book. Then the rabbi began to cry. The abbot could not contain himself. He covered his face with his hands and began to cry too. For the first time in his life, he cried his heart out. The two men sat there like lost children, filling the hut with their sobs and wetting the wood of the table with their tears.

After the tears had ceased to flow and all was quiet again, the rabbi lifted his head. "You and your brothers are serving God with heavy hearts," he said. "You have come to ask a teaching of me. I will give you a teaching, but you can only repeat it once. After that, no one must ever say it aloud again."

The rabbi looked straight at the abbot and said, "The Messiah is among you." For a while, all was silent. Then the rabbi said, "Now you must go."

The abbot left without a word and without ever looking back.

The next morning, the abbot called his monks together in the chapter room. He told them he had received a teaching from "the rabbi who walks in the woods" and that this teaching was never again to be spoken aloud. Then he looked at each of his brothers and said, "The rabbi said that one of us is the Messiah."

The monks were startled by this saying. "What could it mean?" they asked themselves. "Is brother John the Messiah? Or Father Matthew? Or Brother Thomas? Am *I* the Messiah? What could this mean?"

They were all deeply puzzled by the rabbi's teaching. But no one ever mentioned it again.

As time went by, the monks began to treat one another with a very special reverence. There was a gentle, wholehearted, human quality about them now which was hard to describe but easy to notice. They lived with one another as men who had finally found something. But they prayed the Scriptures together as men who were always looking for something. Occasional visitors found themselves deeply moved by the life of these monks. Before long, people were coming from far and wide to be nourished by the prayer life of the monks and young men were asking, once again, to become part of the community.

In those days, the rabbi no longer walked in the woods. His hut had fallen into ruins. But, somehow or other, the old monks who had taken his teaching to heart still felt sustained by his prayerful presence.[6]

Does not this story tell us the task of the parish, that its role is to whisper to us as we march along that one of us is the Messiah? To enable us to live together as a people "who had finally found something"? To have people draw near in our liturgies to be nourished by prayer? To form a

Christian community? Finally, to sustain others by his or her prayerful incarnational presence? That's the story every parish not only wants to tell, but wants to be.

3

This final section is a transition to the next part where we hope to identify practical elements which translate all that we have so far seen into practice. Now, granted we could have approached such practical elements in an entirely different way. Ours is not necessarily the best or the most effective. Yet we choose the way of sacrament-sign and American revivalism because I believe that in their way they encapsulate the general rhythms of Christian history, development, and tensions of the past two thousand years. Furthermore I feel that such a close-to-home sociological framework gives us the broad context we need to talk about the parish in real life. Here briefly, then, are some principles drawn from the previous pages and counterpointed against the primitive church in Acts, which will form the material for the next part of this book.

1. *The parish must take its sign value seriously.* To discover what we mean, ask yourself what are the associations when someone says "St. Joseph's parish" or "St. Robert's parish" (or name your own parish). What does it stand for? What is it known as, famous (or infamous) for? Is it a sacramental sign of Christ or a symbol of industry, power, and money? If the parish is that small but essential Christ-sign, a sacrament of his Risen Presence, then we must try to make it precisely that. We must examine it to see if it promotes the values and celebrates well the ancient Christian symbols that give meaning and hope to human life. And in its seeking to be a relevant sign the parish must be traditional

enough so that it projects a touchbase with ancient foundations, and it must be progressive enough in that it simply does not pass down tradition like some inert mass, but adds to it, draws from it and organically moves through it to be relevant to current needs. We recall in the primitive church the momentous move into the Gentile world. It was made only by finding in Jesus' own reaching out to the outcasts of his society, the fringe people, the principle to move beyond Palestinian Jewish forms of Christianity. By reaching back to touch base with Christ the early church validated its move to new ways and to the future. Every parish must be like that: rooted in Christ, ready to move into the future. So it has its choice of what kind of sign of Jesus it will be. Shall it be a citadel of unchangeableness, a service station for grace-dispensing, or an alive community where the gospel values can be a foundation for a people to discover who they are in a highly pluralistic world? Shall it be an institutional building on the corner or the gathering where one celebrates the Spirit of Christ through its service, fellowship, and liturgy? Shall it be another competitive business venture or a living ministry of hope bearing common witness? As Henri Nouwen says:

> It is in the midst of this dark world that the Christian community is being tested. Can we be light, salt, and leaven to our brothers and sisters in the human family? Can we offer hope, courage, and confidence, to the people of this era? Can we break through the paralyzing fear by making those who watch us exclaim, "See how they love each other, how they serve their neighbor, and how they pray to their Lord"? Or do we have to confess that at this juncture of history we just do not have the needed strength or the generosity and that our Christian communities are little more than sodalities of well-intentioned people supporting each other in their individual interests?[7]

If Christ is the point then the image the parish projects is vital and critically related to the sacramental principle.

2. *The parish must take revivalism seriously.* In time of stress, such as we are going through, secular and religious groups proliferate. They are all basically variations on the same theme: the search for meaning and value to life. Historically, it has always been that way. The most colorful developments in Christian community have emerged in times of crises when forms of society were changing.[8] Such developments are usually religiously nonconforming and catch hold of some basic gospel message that has been lost or downplayed. To that extent such movements, such revivalisms have something to say to us. They can bring new forms and understandings to the parish, even when they themselves eventually go too far or fall into fanaticism. It is easy to laugh at or dismiss such groups or movements that do so, but we would be simplistically wrong not to read in them some message for ourselves. Revivalisms have been part and parcel of Christianity, and the larger issues of which they are symptomatic and the peculiar gospel message they tend to overemphasize have something to tell a complacent church or parish. If nothing else, their very existence and the very strength of their following ought to challenge the parish.

I would venture to say that the particular challenge revivalism issues to us is to refocus our vision. Most of us were brought up on parish bureaucratic officialdom and its demands. Now the revival urges us to a fundamental discovery of Christ again. As Bernard Cooke says, we are being pushed to move from questions of church membership, doctrine, and rules, which are important, to the far more important question of Jesus: and who he is and what he means to my life. What we are eventually being pressured into, I feel, is a real shift of emphasis away from the church as institution to church as Christ-revealing, Christ-bearing, Christ-challenging. In this sense to take the best of revivalism seriously is to take up its search for the person of Christ.

3. *The parish must take eschatology seriously.* Eschatology means simply that we are future oriented, that we look forward to the fulfillment of the kingdom which in fact includes the second coming of Christ. By now we have lost the only prayer we have recorded from the primitive church, "Maranatha" which means, "Come, Lord Jesus." Two thousand years of delay have understandably dulled that expectation. Plus we have grown cautious of those strange, starry-eyed fanatics who are always heading up the nearest mountain top to await the grand show of global destruction with sometimes undisguised glee. Still, such weird people aside, they are potent reminders that the second coming is a genuine part of our tradition, that we are on an unfulfilled journey, and that we live in expectation. Even our eucharist tells us that. St. Paul says that "every time, then, you eat this bread and drink this cup, you proclaim the death of the Lord *until he comes.*" The eucharist not only celebrates the presence of the Risen Christ, but looks forward to his second coming. So we are not an already self-fulfilled enterprise as a Catholic church: we are instead (as the first chapter told us) a part of the larger kingdom of God straining for completion and fulfillment in the Christ "who will come again to judge the living and the dead." Of course we can't go around with those cartoon signs proclaiming that the end is near but, as Christians, to live in the tension of the now and the yet-to-come is critical to our faith. We may smirk at all those wild souls forever shouting doomsday or calculating calendar dates for Christ's return, but we should take seriously the core of their message. We should understand our parish

life as a place where the eucharistic community gathers to proclaim the death of the Lord until he comes, but a death which saves and makes that coming, not a time of fear, but of happy expectation which leads us once more to cry out "Maranatha!"

A word of caution: this very expectation must lead us to bring the kingdom to fulfillment, and this puts the burden on us to strive for social justice. It does not provide us with an excuse to ignore this world's needs. Beyond that, we can just briefly remark that such traditional Christian stances as poverty and celibacy derive much of their meaning against an eschatological background. They are sharp, dissonant reminders in a materialistic world that expectation of the second coming and the realities of the kingdom are not myths of the movies, but myths of the gospel.

4. *The parish must take the charismatic movements seriously.* Here I mean by charismatic groups like the cursillo and marriage encounter and *folcolari* as well as the organized charismatic renewal movement that is so popular. We may be justified in having some reservations about such movements but, as we have seen, they are part and parcel of our church history and our national history and they are always telling us something. In fact, the plain truth is that the church started out as a Spirit-filled community; it began as a charismatic experience. Karl Rahner says that "the charismatic belongs to the essence of the church just as necessarily and permanently as do hierarchial office and the sacraments."[9] We see the open-ended enthusiasm in the first Pentecost, the dramatic result of the inner experience of being born again, being baptized in the Spirit. The utter joy and freedom is very evident.

But we see something else in the New Testament as well: it is the quick need to bring some order into the freewheeling charisms of the people. In fact, it is no exaggeration to say that the history of the early church is one big struggle to bring some form and stability to the first enspirited communities. It is no accident that Matthew has Jesus say, for example, "But not everyone who says to me 'Lord, Lord' will enter the kingdom" or those who claimed to have worked miracles in his name. This is scoring a point in Matthew's church community against that enthusiastic piety which thinks of itself as the sole bearer of wonder-working powers beyond or against that community. St. Paul in his epistle to the Corinthians is clearly trying to head off the dangers of uncontrolled enthusiasms. John's epistles show us the problems of a totally spirit-led community with no human, episcopal authority; it simply disintegrates. By the third generation of Christians it is evident that John's communities must accept or develop some kind of structure or perish. The author of the *Didache,* written at the end of the first century, expresses concern over uncontrolled enthusiasts and prophets also. He lays down the injunction that every wandering prophet is welcomed for a day but that after that he should leave. Maybe he or she may be permitted to stay for three days longer but, beyond that, "he is a false prophet." It is clear that the author prefers a more stable structure of bishop and deacon to the erratic enthusiast.[10] This is why the bishop was introduced as head of the community: to be a focal point of structure and to bring order. Scholar Hans Lietzmann reminds us that by the end of the second century such charismatic enthusiasm had finally been brought under the control of the institution. "From the saying, 'The church is where the spirit is,' the struggle with gnosticism led to the new thesis: 'The church is where the bishop is.' . . . The Spirit revealed himself now . . . not as formerly in prophets and those who spoke in tongues, but in the bishop and the clergy whom the bishop led. . . ."[11] Ernest

Kasemann goes so far as to say that "the theological and practical conquest of enthusiasm was the first test to which the young church was exposed, and nothing less than its whole existence and future depended on its mastery of this problem."[12]

So the institution eventually triumphed over the charismatic; still it never succeeded in displacing it altogether and in fact it should not. And when the institution became too much institution, then the original Spirit impulse would take hold and reassert itself. All throughout our history the evidence of this is abundant. In our day, in our lingering antiinstitutionalism, enspirited prophets and movements, such as the charismatic renewal, are authentic voices of that tradition which goes back to the first Pentecostal experience to call us back to our foundations. Discernment is needed to tell the genuine from false voices, but like the author of the *Didache* we must be very hesitant in simply writing them all off lest we sin against the Spirit.[13] The lesson for the parish in all of this is clear. It must not be so free that it has no order but not so institutionalized that it allows no prophets to speak in word or deed.

5. *The parish must take pluralism and ecumenism seriously.* This means a pluralism of positions, a pluralism of ministries, a pluralism of authority, and a pluralism of approaches in liturgy, organization, and theology. It is noteworthy, for example, that in our first recorded tension in the primitive church (Acts 6:1–7) the apostles would not get involved. Nor would they impose one single answer. Instead they simply suggested that the people settle the matter themselves concerning favored or neglected widows by picking their own presbyter-bishops (not deacons as often misunderstood) to look after the matter. We note too that the primitive church contained, even if

uneasily at times, the conservative James, the middle of the road Peter, and the liberal Paul. Some Jewish Christians were very much for the Jewish Temple,[14] others very much against but they could coexist in unity for belief in Jesus superseded all their differences. Later in church life we find revealing remarks over the Easter date controversy. One third-century writer comments that "in most of the other provinces much is different in accordance with the variation of places and of men. Yet for that reason no one is ever torn from the peace and unity of the Catholic Church." (That is a nice quote for those Catholics who still maintain about their favorite thing: "But it's always been that way!") Another writer looking at the same Easter date controversy a few years later has occasion to remark, "Everyone was to celebrate the feast as he had been accumstomed to, without thereby being cut off from reciprocal communion.... One cannot find the same traditions—equal in every respect—in all churches, even when they enjoy the same faith."[15]

In the Middle Ages we see an amazing variety of theological opinion set forth with great vigor in the famous university debates among the Franciscans and Dominicans and other later orders. Even Luther's ninety-five theses posted on the sixteenth-century church door caused no doctrinal upheaval as such. There was nothing in them that legitimately could not be debated or discussed. The medieval church was wrapped around with varieties of custom, order, age, and gender.[16] Only nearer our time, with the rise of modernism and the fears of Pius X and his conservative curia, did pluralism narrow down to a party line in everything. Today, however, a shrinking planet has opened our eyes to the rich variety that is the universal church, East and West, and given us a new appreciation for the many-sided approaches to Jesus and his gospel. In fact, the current vast expansiveness of the church into the southern hemisphere, in Africa, South America, and Asia has given us a whole new respect for the variety of cultural approaches to the faith and church leadership has wisely honored them. The local parish must therefore reflect this new pluralism within its collective life. At least it must not be so rigid that it is closed to new forms and organizations and to a measurable degree of variety, sharing, and decentralization.

As for ecumenism, if the church, as we have seen, is the servant of the world and not its only means of salvation; if it has a subsidiary function to play, not a dominating one, then practical ecumenism is upon us. Again, as we have indicated, not in the sense of abandoning the faith or making it "one among equals" nor blunting the assertions of Jesus who said he was "the way and the truth and the life," but in style, approach, and tolerance. Cultural imperialism and triumphalism are gone, leaving us to acquire the respect and humility to assent to these words of Abraham Joshua Heschel:

> I suggest that the most significant basis for the meeting of men of different religious traditions is the level of fear and trembling, of humility and contrition, where our individual moments of faith are mere waves in the endless ocean of mankind's reaching out for God, where all formulations and articulations appear as understatements, where our souls are swept away by the awareness of the urgency of answering God's commandment, while stripped of pretension and conceit we sense the tragic insufficiency of human faith.[17]

So much for the principles the parish ought to take seriously. We are now ready to move to Part II, to explore together there the immediate practical applications of these principles and how they are translated into the four foundations of the creative parish.

Notes for Chapter 4

1. Andrew Greeley, "Catholicism in America: Two Hundred Years and Counting," *The Critic* 34. no. 4. (Summer 1976) p. 42.
2. M. Scott Peck, M.D. *The Road Less Travelled* (Simon and Schuster, 1978), p. 89.
3. Monica Furlong, *Travelling In* (London: Hodder and Stoughton, 1971), p. 17.
4. *Parobola* IV: 1, (February 1979), p. 3.
5. Franz Kafka, "An Imperial Message" (Schocken Books, 1948).
6. Francis Dorff, "The Rabbi's Gift," *The New Catholic World* (March/April 1979), p. 53.
7. Henri J. M. Nouwen, *Clowning in Rome* (Image Books, 1979), p. 8.
8. See William J. Bausch, *Pilgrim Church,* rev. ed. (Fides/Claretian, 1977), ch. XIV.
9. Quoted in Edward D. O'Connor *The Pentecostal Movement in the Catholic Church* (Ave Maria Press, 1971), p. 282.
10. *The Didache,* Ancient Christian Writers, No. 6 (Newman Press, 1948), 11 to 15.
11. Hans Lietzmann, *The Founding of the Church Universal* (Meridian, 1963), pp. 54-61. See also Ernest Kasemann *New Testament Questions of Today* (Fortress Press, 1969), ch. IV.
12. Ernest Kasemann, *Perspective on Paul* (Fortress Press, 1971), p. 123. That the church (nervously) feels that this "problem" must be continually mastered is evident in Vatican II's statement: "Judgment as to the genuineness and the proper use of the charisms belongs to those who preside over the church and to whose special competence it belongs, not indeed to extinguish the Spirit, but to test all things and hold fast to that which is good" (*Lumen Gentium,* n. 12).
13. *The Didache,* 11:7.
14. For an anti-Temple attitude see John's account of the woman at Jacob's well. Note the words Jesus says there (Jn 4). See James D. G. Dunn, *Unity and Diversity in the New Testament* (Westminster Press, 1977).

15. Firmilian of Caesarea writing to St. Cyprian.

16. See Bausch, *Pilgrim Church,* ch. XV, especially pp. 313–14. See also Robert L. Kinast, "Principles for the Pastoral Use of Pluralistic Theology," *Chicago Studies* 18, no. 2 (Summer 1979), pp. 197ff., and Jaroslav Pelikan, *The Growth of Medieval Theology* (600–1300) (University of Chicago Press, 1978), vol. 3.

17. Quoted in E. Glenn Hinson, "Expansive Catholicism: Ecumenical Perceptions of Thomas Merton," *Religion in Life* 48 (Spring 1979), p. 63.

PART II

FOUNDATIONS OF THE CREATIVE PARISH

5. Ministry, A and The

1

We all remember the four marks of the church: one, holy, catholic, and apostolic. It was the way, we were taught, to tell the true (ours) from the counterfeit (theirs) church of Jesus Christ. They are still pretty good signs though used today in a different way as the first chapter indicated. In these next chapters I should like to discuss what I call the four marks of the creative parish. Because we are going through our own great awakening and are in the process of confusion, therapy, and eventual restoration we want to see, however darkly, where we're going or, more properly, discern where the Spirit is taking us. These four marks, while far from infallible are offered as signposts of what the future might be or at least what the present parish should be becoming in its current evolution. It might be best to outline the four marks here and then describe each one in turn:

THE CREATIVE PARISH		THE UNCREATIVE PARISH
	versus	
I. Ministry: shared between A and The		Solo performance by clergy

II. Vision & Spirituality	Service Station to "save souls"
III. Wide Scope: singles, divorced and separated, families, alienated, etc.	Narrow programs and organizations (mostly from the past)
IV. Social Justice	Same as II: add "for members only"

It is these four marks which, I believe, are the four pillars on which rests a truly creative parish. They at least bear investigation as material to build on no matter which way we rearrange or expand them. First, then, to ministry.

2

May 1st to 3rd of 1979 may not be remembered as great dates in world history, but for us they have symbolic significance. On those dates a special information report prepared by the U.S. Bishops' Committee on Doctrine was presented to the bishops at their Chicago meeting. It concerned the difference between the ordained and lay ministry, a topic that has become quite crucial in our times. The first issue tackled was an attempt to clarify meanings:

> In defining ministry one must keep in mind that it is above all the response to the call to serve that Christ makes to the entire church. As history shows, this service is always open to further exploration and understanding. . . . The original Greek word *diakonia* is used in the New Testament in a rather broad sense. . . . In the course of time, the meaning of the word, especially in Latin usage, was restricted so that it referred only to the ordained. *Ministerium* applied generically to all activity

of the ordained and another translation from the Greek, *dioconatus,* became the specific name of the third within the group of episcopacy, presbyterium, and diaconate. Two shortcomings can be noted in this evolution of a concept. First of all, the use of the term for the ordained ministry meant in great part that little account was taken, in practice and in theory, of the mission of the laity. Secondly, the word's connotations often became those of power rather than of humility and service.

In this century, Vatican II signaled a new beginning, which had already started to take shape some years before the Council. The ecclesiology of the conciliar documents is one which gives first place to the mission of the church. It then recognized the active part which all who have received the sacraments of initiation play in this life and in this mission. In this context, it draws attention to the way in which the gifts of the Spirit determine the contribution of each member. In the third place, it introduces the role of the ordained in the leadership of the church.

Naturally, it was not easy to find a perfectly harmonious way in which to express both the ministry of the laity and the ministry of the ordained, as well as their reciprocal relationship. Speaking of both, the Council emphasized that all ministry and all power in the church are rooted in the loving service and humility to which Jesus Christ called his disciples, and in the mission and ministry of Christ himself.

The short document (we will have to amplify the last paragraph later) then goes on to say that we need to explore the relationship of the ministries, ordained and lay, but in the meantime we should not forget that the Council (1) emphasized the responsibility of *all* the baptized in the mission of the church, (2) spoke of the need to explore the gifts of the laity, (3) demanded courage and openness on the part of the ordained segment, and (4) said that practical pluralism as ministries developed would have to be noted and studied. These words are a kind of capsule of what's been happening to make the late 1970s truly the "time of the laity." It speaks of roots and history and theology and so, once again, we ought to look at the origins of the question.

The term laity today means nonclergy or, in a wide sense, nonprofessional. This is a long, long way from its biblical roots which tell another, more profound story (one being recaptured today). The Old Testament used the word *laos* or laity as referring to the whole people, that is, Israel. So Israel takes on the meaning of an entire people called by God. All of Israel, the *laos* are a people chosen by the Lord, are his possession, "You shall be my own possession among all the people; for all the earth is mine and you shall be to me a kingdom of priests and a holy nation . . . and all the people answered together and said, 'All that the Lord has spoken we will do'" (Ex 19:4–7). So Israel, the people, the whole nation as a unit is the *laos,* called to service as the Lord's chosen vessel, to full ministry, to full priesthood. Even the later developed Hebrew priesthood does not only not negate the priesthood of the whole nation, but works precisely to enable that people to be what they have been called to.

Now it is *this* notion of *laos* which passes into the New Testament vocabulary and concept. Its best description is given by the author of 1 Peter: "You are a chosen race, a royal priesthood, a holy nation. . . . Once you were no people but now you are God's people . . . " (2:9, 10). In other words, the Christian community, also in its entirety, as a full assembly, is the new *laos* or people of God. Priesthood and its responsibilities are therefore assigned to the whole *laos.* This does not mean, however, that there is no room for leadership and special ministries. Remember that its "priesthood of the people" did not prevent Israel from instituting a special cultic priesthood. So with the first church. Being a "chosen race and royal priesthood" did not prevent it from doing the same. There was never a wholly democratic, structureless church. We saw before that such charismatic elan was quickly structured for the sake of order and stability. All scholars say that we find in the New Testament a Petrine ministry, an episcopal ministry, and a presbyterial ministry. Their jobs are not necessarily what we have come to think of today, but they are there and ordination was involved. In fact, in time, such ordinations were considered vital enough to be raised to the dignity of a sacrament.

However, what we want to stress is that we find ordination was not primary (not unimportant, just not primary). The fact was that the clergy (if we want to call them that for the sake of discussion) themselves were members and remained members of the *laos,* the laity, as indeed they are today. They are fundamentally laity who have a special ministry within the laity. Being an ordained minister is not *the* ministry, but *a* ministry, one among many. The whole people of God, the church, remain the basic priesthood, taking up their collective task of witnessing and celebrating. The publically ordained ministry enables this to happen by giving it focus through word and sacrament. Therefore, in the words of the World Conference of Faith and Order held in Montreal in 1963, "every special ordained minister of the church is and remains first of all a baptized member of the church. He or she continues to belong to the laity . . . to belong to God's *laos,* to God's people. It is therefore wrong to define the laity over against especially ordained ministers and vice versa. However, the basic ordination of baptism does not exclude subsequent ordinations for special tasks. It is possible and necessary to distinguish within the total baptized membership of the church persons who have been 'set apart' through a special ordination for a special task."[1] That, in fact, was the way St. Paul described himself in his opening lines in the epistle to the Romans, "Paul, the servant of Christ Jesus, apostle by God's call, set apart for the service of the gospel" (1:1). This "setting apart" does have its collective impact and witness when it is seen, not as substitute for the inactivity of other Christians, but as an extension of the faith community's action and ministry. To receive a particular recognition through ordination or commissioning is to give special focus to the whole corporate enterprise of the church. The visible, public structure of ordination is an important and needed sign of what the whole church is about, a symbolic emphasis of the whole church's mission.

Obviously we've come a long way from the ordained ministry being *a* ministry to its being *the* ministry, with the resulting diminished meaning of the word laity. We've come a long way from certain members of the laity being ordained to the ministry of cult to becoming members of a caste. The genesis of this division goes back in Christian history. Quite early, for example, the bishop's role in the rather fluid structure of the Christian community becomes distinct. Gradually it overshadowed the larger presbyterate governing body and eventually merged into the single-rule (monarchial) bishop of the community. By the end of the second and third centuries we find this one-bishop rule common. This prominence in turn brought increasing attention to the catagories of the ordained ministry. At the beginning of the third century we find the first full, written description of an ordination ritual for bishops, presbyters, and deacons. As yet there is no intent of superiority or separateness, only function. They were still too near to St. Paul's words to have it otherwise: "Now there are varieties of gifts, but the same Spirit; and there are varieties of service, but the same Lord. . . . To each is given the manifestation of the Spirit for the common good. . . . Now you are the body of Christ and individually members of it. And God has appointed in the church first apostles, second prophets, third teachers, then workers of miracles, then healers, helpers administrators, speakers in various kinds of tongues" (1 Cor 12:4–6; 27–30). However, the very emphasis on an ordination ritual does portend the beginning of an unbalanced focus on ordination rather than on baptism as the supreme symbol of the common Christian calling.

An even earlier hint of what would evolve into separateness is found in the works of Clement of Rome. He was writing at the end of the first century and therefore at the same time as the authors of the later books of the New Testament. For the very first time in Christian writings the word laity is mentioned as a distinct catagory. Clement says, "Special functions are assigned to the high priest; a special office is imposed upon the priests; and special ministrations fall to the Levites. The layman is bound by the rules laid down for the laity" (*Epistle to the Corinthians,* 40:5). His contemporary, Ignatius of Antioch, also makes a distinction between laity and clergy (*Letter to the Ephesians,* 4:2). This ancient distinction is reflected in Vatican II's words that the official priesthood is distinguished from the common priesthood of the faithful "in essence and not only in degree." In other words, while the whole church, the *laos,* is the tangible and visible representation of the priesthood of Christ, the particular priesthood of the clergy is an activity within that general priesthood. It is not opposed to it nor does it diminish the priestly character of the people of God; it is a particular expression within it. Therefore Clement and Ignatius, and the early church in general, did not intend the word priest to evoke any special response. Nor would they use the term in connection with any human individual to denote the unique mediator between God and man, for they knew well enough that there is only one mediator-priest: Jesus Christ. The epistle to the Hebrews taught them that. That is why the word priest is nowhere to be found in the New Testament in reference to a Christian individual. That is why this special priesthood was not seen as opposed to the general priesthood—that would come into Christianity around the fourth century, for sooner or later distinctions tend to apartness and caste; rather the term related to a particular ministry not necessarily a superior one.

The same was true of the bishop. He too was among the laity. He lived and worked with them. He was truly a laity of the laity, an important enabling minister among the many nonordained ministers that flourished in the early church. The bishops were not a self-perpetuating, self-regulating body that could exist independently of community choice. They were a people publicly accountable to the community whose life and tradition they served. St. Augustine of the fifth century said it handsomely and profoundly; "What I am for you terrifies me, what I am with you, consoles me. For you I am a bishop, but with you I am a Christian. The former is a title of duty; the latter, one of grace. . . . The former is a danger; the latter, salvation."

Let us take note now of a certain terminology which, gracious as it sounds, creeps in at this time and widens the gap between the "clergy" and the "laity." It is the phrase "Mother Church" and the notion of "Shepherd" bishop. If the church is a mother then it is somehow distinct from the average layperson who must be taken care of, nourished, fed, and "mothered" by the leaders. We find this patronizing tendency escalating in post-Nicene times when the bishops become civil functionaries as well as spiritual leaders. Even the elders and presbyters begin to lose their independence and eventually dwindle into helpers or extensions of the bishops. Before long, Christian ministry slips into questions of power, authority and control. Collaboration, once the ideal, now turns into submission. Further cleavage between the ordained and nonordained ministries is aggravated by steady clerical exemptions from civil service, taxes, law suits, and by clerical celibacy. All of this slow but steady development is having its effect on the community. It is being hammered into a pyramid from its original circle.

Liturgically, too, we can find evidence of a growing cleavage. It was the sixth-century notion of "sacredos," priesthood which evolved into the notion of mediator between the people of God, which implied that the priest is the sole agent of the sacred action and that he is doing it on behalf of the people—not with them. So much does this catch hold that by the eighth century the *laos,* or laity, has been reduced to almost total silence at worship and the canon is said quietly for, in the words of Bernard Cooke, "only the celebrant needs to know what is being said or needs to express his sacrificing intent. The celebrant is the high priest offering sacrifice on behalf of the people rather than the *leitourgos* of a sacrificing community; he is the sacred actor performing the mystery rite, rather than the prophetic herald of the redeeming gospel of Christ's death and resurrection."[2] Add to this the impact of the various reform movements throughout the centuries. They came primarily (and nobly) from the clergy of the monasteries. While they did marvelous and much-needed work, they brought to the reform and to the church at large monastic ideals and concepts which are basically nonministerial, a certain passive prayer life and acceptance and inner spirituality, all of which had the net effect of making the clergy the active part of the church and the people the passive part. We can see this most easily perhaps in the whole development of the etiquette of the sacraments using language to this day which connotes the active-clergy versus passive-laity roles. "The Most Reverend Bishop will administer the sacrament of Confirmation in our parish in November" (not he will celebrate it with the community in November; he will give, inject, administer, bring it, and spoon it out to his children). "Father baptizes, or anoints, or "says" Mass.

Perhaps a key hardening of clerical-lay positions came in the twelfth century when certain movements reacted against the now well-established hierarchial system (hierarchy means literally "rule by priests"). The old theory of conciliarism was brought forth more forcefully proclaiming that a democratic general council was higher than any pope, bishop, or priest. The theory was an open attack on the hierarchial structure and so provoked the strong counterattack which we have inherited. This counterattack left us with the established insistence on a multileveled church structure reaching downward from the pinacle of the papacy, through the bishops and the pastors to the bottom-runged laity whose chief duty was expressed in the witticism of "pay, pray, and obey." Thus did counterattack theology consecrate the pyramid symbol of the church and standardize the terms clergy and laity. Moreover, when the first catechisms appeared in the sixteenth century they spoke of salvation as being mediated only through the structure of popes, bishops, and priests. The laity were pictured as recipients. Post-Trent theology unfortunately did not find its base in the confessing assembly of the *laos* or its local expression, the parish, but in a firm doctrinal stance and a particular style of teaching. This posture of strict clerical-lay divisions held the field and in fact was blessed by Vatican I and such papal encyclicals as Pius XII's influential *Mystici Corporis.* Even the first draft of Vatican II on the church carried this old theology. Fortunately, this first draft was rejected. A very different definition of the church was proposed, accepted, and is having its creative explosions right now.

3

What *did* Vatican II say? It said things like this: "The lay apostolate is a participation in the saving mission of the church itself. Through their baptism and confirmation, all are commissioned to that apostolate by the Lord himself," and "These faithful are by baptism made one body with Christ and are established among the people of God. They are, in their own way, made sharers in the priestly, prophetic, and kingly functions of Christ. They carry out their own part in the mission of the whole Christian people with respect to the church and the world."[3] And, finally a gentle nudge to priests: "Pastors also know that they themselves were not meant by Christ to shoulder alone the entire saving mission of the church towards the world. On the contrary, they understand that it is their noble duty so to shepherd the faithful and recognize their services and charismatic gifts, that all according to their proper role may cooperate in this common undertaking with one heart." The recent declaration, *Evangelization in the Modern World* repeats the motif: "The whole church receives the mission to evangelize and the work of each individual is important for the whole.... Having been sent and evangelized, the church herself sends evangelizers."

Now it would be nice to say that we have entered the

Promised Land where we are all blended into one cooperative *laos* once more, each with his several gifts, but hammering that pyramid back into the circle is going to be hard work, fraught with dangers and in need of much patience and clarity on all sides. So there are several principles and clarifications we must explore in this section if we are at least to get started in the right direction.

The first principle is to be more precise. So far, in order to make the points about the entire *laos* aspect of the church and Vatican II's insistence that we are all called to the mission of Jesus, we have gone along with the popular blurring of words. Now more precision is needed. It was that precision sought after, you might recall, in the opening pages of this chapter in the statement of the bishops' Chicago meeting. The last paragraph said, "Naturally, it was not easy to find a perfectly harmonious way in which to express both the ministry of the laity and the ministry of the ordained as well as their reciprocal relationship. . . ." The document is right and we will probably reflect this difficulty by continuing to use the term "ministry" quite loosely. Still, for the time being (even though we slip into loose talk later) we should attempt some distinctions. If we do not we will wind up so emasculating the word ministry that it will become useless. That would be regretable for it is a firm word in its own right.

Let us start by saying that the word ministry should not refer to *anything* a Christian does. We really should not speak of the ministry of hairdressing or the ministry of shoeshining or the ministry of dishwashing. Ministry has a stronger, more biblical meaning than that. Richard Dillon in an article entitled "Ministry as Stewardship in the Tradition of the New Testament,"[4] after surveying all of the New Testament ministries, defines the term as "stewardship of the tradition." Bernard Cooke uses five categories to describe ministry: formation of community, ministry to God's word, service to the people, ministry to God's judgment, and ministry to the church's sacramentality.[5] Henri Nouwen gives his five categories describing ministry as teaching, preaching, individual pastoral care, organizing the community, and celebrating.[6] Whatever description we use, the point that any such listings makes is that, in our tradition, ministry is a fairly restricted term. It means much more than the general witnessing everyone is supposed to give anyway in virtue of his or her baptism. So there must be distinctions made. We would suggest the following divisions for clarification—at least until the church gives us better guides:

1. Laos
2. Laity
3. Ministry which is divided into
    (a) nonordained
    (b) ordained

The first word *laos* we have seen enough. We will mention it and promptly forget it for no one is going around speaking Greek. The word refers, as we have seen, to the overall idea that all of us are in the common, united venture of the ministry of Jesus. It is mentioned here as the first of our divisions to suggest all of the historical and theological background we have reviewed in the past pages. It is mentioned as a further reminder that the means of salvation are not concentrated in the hands of a few.

The second word in our outline, laity, is associated with the key words of mission and witness. That is, every baptized person, by virtue of that baptism, is called to witness individually to the work of Christ in his church. There is a necessary strong element of spirituality implied here: a growing in the intimacy of Jesus and bringing his grace-fullness to one's everyday life in work, application, and decision. The task is not delegated by an ecclesiastical system; this mission is not clerically given nor are the laity set apart thereby from the community. On the contrary, the ministries of mission and witness belong to the lay people as lay people and are exercised by them in their own right. Here, if you will, is the "ministry" of hairdressing, shoe-shining, and dishwashing—and a host of other everyday vocations. Each one's experience and personal charism will prompt him here. There is no professional schooling needed, no training, no official set-apartness; just the glorious grace of the daily gospel dulled by familiarity.

The third word is ministry properly so called, and it has two divisions or categories. Both categories—and here is the critical distinction from the preceding *laos* and laity—are called and set apart explicitly or implicitly by the community. The first category of the nonordained ministry is one conferred by installation or commissioning. To that extent it is officially designated by the church. This does not necessarily mean, however, a personal document from the pope or bishop—though this does happen in the case of eucharistic ministers—or some hierarchially inspired ceremony, but it does mean two things. It means either an explicit designating of certain people by the community for some task, this designation taking the form of some public commissioning or installation ceremony in the parish church. Or it may mean an implicit response by some people to a real community need that the community recognizes, calls for, and is quite conscious of even without some public ceremony. Such might be the case, for example, where there is a sudden need to deal with and care for senior citizens. All the parish is aware of this need, and certain people just naturally respond to it by temperament or training. They are noted for such work, recognized as being associated with it by all the parish and in the name of the parish, even though no public ceremony of commissioning has taken place. Usually implied in all of this, for the people so involved, is some background and training, spiritual formation, and a certain openness to accountability to the parish or the pastor or the parish council. Perhaps even a measure of parish financing is involved. The point is that some kind of officialness is here and, most often (and wisely) a public recognition in a public installation or a commissioning ceremony. Such a ceremony or commissioning is not only important for the nonordained ministry properly so called but practical as well: it keeps the corporate discernment open and prevents solo flights into fantasy; it gives the community a handle on the deluded.

The second category of ministry is that conferred, not by installation or commissioning, but by ordination. As the Asian Bishops' Conference expresses it:

> The apostolic ministry of leadership belongs to the essential structure of the church. It is now embodied in the college of bishops, into which individual bishops are inscribed by episcopal ordination. From the early tradition the ministry of leadership, whose specific function is to signify in the community the headship of Jesus over his church, has taken on two additional forms in the ministries of the presbyterate and the diaconate. Common to the three forms of the ministry conferred by ordination, though differently realized in each, is a charism of unity and spiritual leadership.

This is the ministry related to the sacrament of orders. Those laity so ordained are given power and mandated by ecclesiastical authority. They are officially inserted into the church structure, and their association is such that they no longer speak for themselves but now belong to the public forum.

At this point we can return to our outline and flesh it out somewhat:

1. Laos: the whole church as the presence and work of Jesus. These are the total:
2. Laity: all those called to mission and witness in virtue of baptism prompted by experience and personal charism. Some of this laity exercises:
3. Ministry:
   (a) the nonordained laity but those explicitly or implicitly installed, commissioned, recognized and held to accountability.
   (b) laity ordained into the public forum of ecclesiastical structure. (This has no necessary implication about the sex of the laity so ordained, but more of this later.)

It is evident that the three are the one church which in its own right has a variety of expressions.

4

If, as columnist James Reston has said, "religion is too serious a business to be left to the clergy," then the second principle and clarification we must deal with is cooperation. This is the cooperation between the ordained and the nonordained ministries. This is easier said than done. The temptation for a long time, I fear, will be to see the issues in terms of who's-in-charge-here, the issue of power. It is true that the U.S. Catholic Conference document *As One Who Serves* says that "ministry . . . is a vocation, privilege, and responsibility of all members of the church. The ministry of the church is a shared responsibility carried out by all members under the inspiration of the Spirit, according to their particular calling, gift, and competence. All who live in faith are 'gift-ed; and all are called to serve ministry. . . ." But the picture has been lopsided for so long that there is bound to be strain, stress and a crisis of identity for someone.

And uncertainty. We are so *used* to the ordained clergy running things and being the active members of the church. We are so used to being run that we are unsure where to begin and uncertain as to how far we can go. Perhaps we should see Ivan Illich's comment that there are too many full-time workers in the ecclesiastical institution, too many priests and ministers, as challenging rather than cynical. We might read his point to say that only with the depletion of its clerical ranks (such as is happening now) will the church be forced to free itself from the clerical domination which obscures its fundamentally shared mission—something which will be realized, in the blunt words of one writer, "only if the nonclergy are willing to move up, if the clergy are willing to move over, and if all of God's people are willing to move out to bear witness to the common enterprise of the gospel."[7]

And it's no use looking to the other denominations for help. They have the same problems. Writes one of their number, "Although all the churches from the Roman Catholic to the Pentecostal and back again, have worked out a theology of the partnership between clergy and laity, the psychology of the partnership is still very delicate, and it is not easy to have an open and helpful discussion on this point. . . . The word laity is not helpful either—though we have no better one. . . ."[8] Perhaps the metaphor of "the flowering of ministries" might be comforting and useful because ministries really have to be rooted in the nourishing soil of the community, they have to be allowed to grow in their own time and at their own pace. With time, hopefully, the relationship among all the ministries, old and emerging, will be resolved. Signs of this resolution can be found in the cooperation between some religious orders and lay men and women working side by side in some common project. The Capuchins, for example, to demonstrate the concept of *laos,* have changed the name of their lay order from the Third Order of St. Francis to the Secular Order. They want to dissolve any implication that the monastic model which they live is the sole model of ministry and holiness, and that the secular branch is somehow in "third place." Many lay people are engaged in "total but temporary" associations with other ministers, ordained and nonordained. They engage in common work and live a common life. Other religious orders are providing structures for the nonordained ministers to get educated in systems other than seminaries and novitiates and assist them in attending other schools of theology and spirituality. It's all an attempt to proclaim that there are many gifts but one Spirit, to advertise that ministry is the common enterprise of all.

Our final principle and clarification comes back to the bland but realistic statement that the lay ministry is theologically and practically here to stay for its time has come. There are simply too many perceptive people like, say, author Abigail McCarthy, who have seriously reflected on the normally accepted view in their lives of bishops, priests, nuns, laymen and finally, laywomen. She writes, "I confess that, originally, I didn't object to that hierarchial order. In fact, I thought it was a fine division of labor. There were all those people with special callings—vocations—to take care of things for me—to take care of worship, education, evangelization. I had only to attend, to receive, and to support. It took a long time to grow into a realization that I am called to the priesthood of the people of God—that I too, have a calling as a *lay person.*"[9] She speaks for many, and the "many" will not let the concept of nonordained ministry die. The laity are too newly conscious that they must move upward from an identity as second-class members of the community of faith to a status of full privilege and responsibility. They, like everyone else, want to perceive a meaning, dignity, and mandated purpose to their religious lives. The lady named Nora in Stud Terkel's *Working* says, "I think most of us are looking for a calling, not a job. Most of us, like the assembly-line worker, have jobs that are too small for our spirit. Jobs are not big enough for people." But the faith should be.

All this, however, brings us to another sensitive point raised by the forty-seven signers of the Chicago Declaration of December, 1977. Here the lay people rightly praised the new concept of themselves as baptized-commissioned priests in the work of the church. What they objected to was the definition of work. What they objected to was that work was being translated "churchy" work, work connected with the sanctuary. They were suspicious that they would wind up as paraclerics. What they missed in this connection was an emphasis on and a theology of the Christian's work in the world, a theology of their daily lives. The pastoral suggestions coming from the bishops seemed designed to make them priests and nuns without portfolio rather than certified priestly people in the work-aday world. Even in the documents of Vatican II lay activity is mostly described in terms of the world and clerical activity in terms of the church. While there are advantages at times to such a distinction, the overall impression is to separate the church from the world and, as a consequence, once more to reinforce the notion that the real church is all clerical.

The same dilemma was illustrated by Ed Marciniak at the National Assembly of the Laity when he quoted a Lutheran layman who wrote, "I am now a sales manager in a major steel company. In almost thirty years of my professional career, my church has never once suggested that there be any type of accounting of my on-the-job ministry to others. My church has never once offered to improve these skills which could make me a better minister, nor has it ever asked if I needed any kind of support in what I was doing. There has never been an inquiry into the types of ethical decisions I must face. . . ." Russell Barta, a Catholic layman, picks up the challenges and asks us, "When was the last time any of us heard a homily reflecting on the meaning of work? Why do so many pastors address their parishioners on Sunday as if the forty hours of work of the previous week was irrelevant to what was going on in the church? How many retreats given in the past year centered on the need for renewal within the various occupations and professions? How many Catholic colleges today require their graduates to have studied the social teachings of the church? Why isn't a fully developed theology of work one of the top priorities of our theologians?"[10] These are significant questions and pose a challenge to the emerging role of the laity. Ed Marciniak counted forty different occupations in the New Testament and challenges the church that "if four evangelists can use ordinary occupations to tell the Christian story, so can those who draft pastoral letters." In the terms we have used he is saying that laypeople want to be grounded in their own proper mission and witness, not in some clericalized formal "ministry," ordained or nonordained. In other words, they don't want to be covertly approached and asked, "Have you ever thought of becoming a priest (nun, brother)?" simply because they take the gospel seriously.

Still, there is a balance to be met here. Delores Lecky, executive director of the Bishops' Secretariat for the Laity says, "My personal view is that the issue of participation is on the continuum from the center of the church to beyond, into the heart of societal structures. In other words, there is a correlation between the extent and quality of lay participation within the church and the motivation of the laity to engage in responsible Christian action in the world."[11] Here is where the parish can play a crucial part by providing a rooted center of communal spirituality. Ministry (to use the word loosely again) is more than mere service, more than getting the laity to recognize their priesthood and getting them to "get out there and do something." Ministry is first getting them to *be* something and, from this being-ness, to see in a new way oneself and one's sacramental impact on the world. "Any program that seeks to promote and develop ministries of lay persons must seek actively to fight the view that ministry is doing a job, or is an avocation, or is doing something for or to someone else. Instead, ministry as a way of life, ministry as enabling and ministry as mutual are the attitudes that must be inculcated. . . . In order for lay ministers to act with the mind and heart of Christ, serious spiritual and attitudinal formation, must be at the heart of every lay ministers' program."[12] In other words, ministry must be grounded in the contemplative stance and in a faith perspective, for unless we see what we should we cannot make visible in ministry our vision. Theodore Rozak has the point of it when he says, "We can now recognize that the fate of the soul is the fate of the social order; that if the spirit within us withers, so too will all the world we build around us." Ministry, in short, must facilitate the movement between God and people and vice versa; it must make "church" happen.

Before we close this chapter there is one word of caution. Lay ministries are indeed springing up all over the place and people are bringing to them enormous good will, commitment, and increasing competencies.[13] They are enrolling in growing numbers in seminars and formational programs. This is as it should be. The caution, however, is the danger of elitism. What if, ironically, these corporate educated and knowledgeable laity wake up one day and find themselves in another mode of clericalism? If elitism springs up the people of God will suffer. An elite is necessary, but an elite of the people and not apart from them, one that is in constant touch. Otherwise a lay cleric can be just as insufferable as a cleric cleric. A most appropriate ending to this chapter is to relate the response of a group of people from a small Brazilian village to the question, "What kind of church do you want?" Here is their answer: "The church is the ordinary faithful, men and women. Certain lay people have become priests or have been named bishops or chosen popes, not in order to give commands, but in order to serve the community of the faithful. Pope John XXIII was a poor Italian peasant. The church is formed by all those who believe. But it is not enough to know that one belongs to a family; one must take up one's place in it and feel responsibility for the growth of that family. Lay people ought more and more to have their voice in the councils of the church, since they are the church."[14]

Notes for Chapter 5

1. Quoted in *Theological Foundations for Ministry,* ed. Ray S. Anderson (Eerdmans, 1979), p. 435.

2. Bernard Cooke, *Ministry to Word and Sacraments* (Fortress Press, 1976), p. 86.

3. The two quotations are from *Lumen Gentium,* numbers 33 and 31, in Chapter IV, all of which should be read.

4. *Catholic Theological Society of America Proceedings* 24 (1969) 10-62.

5. Cooke, *Ministry to Word and Sacraments.*

6. Henri J. M. Nouwen, *Creative Ministry* (Doubleday, 1971).

7. Thomas Gillespie, "The Laity in Biblical Perspective," in *The New Laity,* ed. Ralph D. Bucy (Word Books, 1978). p. 32. See also Joseph Champlin, *The Living Parish* (Ave Maria Press, 1977).

8. Howard Butt with Elliott Wright, *At the Edge of Hope* (Seabury Press, 1978), p. 88

9. Abigail McCarthy, "Creativity and Community-The Lay Responsibility," in *At the Edge of Hope,* p. 86.

10. Russell Barta, "Let Laypersons Minister in the Marketplace" in *St. Anthony Messenger* (March 1979), p. 28. See also Orley Herron, *A Christian Executive in a Secular World* (Thomas Nelson Publishers, 1979).

11. Delores Lecky, *Origins* 8, no. 16 (October 5, 1978), p. 246.

12. Frank Henderson, *Ministries of the Laity* (Canadian Conference of Catholic Bishops, 1978), p. 12.

13. See, for instance, Barbara Kuhn, *The Whole Lay Ministry Catalogue* (Seabury, 1978), James C. Fenhagen, *More Than Wanderers: Spiritual Disciplines for Christian Ministry* (Seabury, 1979), and Robert W. Hovda, *There Are Different Ministries* (The Liturgical Conference, 1975). See also Richard McBrien, "Service + Mission = Ministry," *Today's Parish* (October, 1979). Also, several dioceses have launched full-fledged lay ministries programs.

14. *Cross Currents* (Spring 1976).

6. Ministry and Identity

1

The concept of ministry has gone far beyond the old notion in the fifties of the lay apostolate and Catholic Action. In those days the lay apostolate was defined as "a participation of the laity in the apostolate of the hierarchy." It was Pius X who wrote in one of his encyclicals, "The church is essentially an unequal society. That is, it is a society formed by pastors and flock. . . . As far as the multitude is concerned, they have no other duty than to let themselves be led." We have come a long way from this notion of subordinate relationship. Ministry is a right from baptism, not a privilege of permission. Still, since the whole notion is new, we should try one more approach, one more figure, to catch the spirit of ministry and the relationship between the ordained and nonordained ministers. Liberation theology, with whatever shortcomings it has, has brought forcefully to our attention that believing really cannot be separated from action. In more exact terms, being cannot be separated from doing. Jesus, for example, was not just a divine being become man; he was one who did atonement. Our interest in him, so to speak, is not merely his incarnation but his saving death and resurrection. He is not merely the "Word become flesh" but also "the lamb who takes away the sin of the world." The whole of redemption, in short, involves both being and doing. Both are important. Jesus' "incarnate doing" is the cause of our salvation. In the past, Christianity has been impoverished when people focused too exclusively on Jesus' person and nature; when they relegated him to a passive divine essence and forgot what he taught, did, and underwent on the cross.

Looking at the church can be like that. We can see it just as an institutional body that is, not as a body that also does. Yet, both what it is and what it does are inseparable sides to the same church of Jesus Christ. Surely the church must be what it is and it must be true to itself, but it must also do the work of Christ. At times, however, the emphasis has come down heavily on what the church is and the people who define it rather than on what it does. This means that the ministry of the clergy was seen as critical in maintaining the identity of the church. They were important to preserve the church in its beingness. Active clergy were called upon to proclaim and promote the identifying marks of the church. Passive lay ministers were to respond to and affirm the identity. And how did the clergy do this? By fulfilling the duties of their office: preaching the word of God, proclaiming those traditions, creeds, and liturgies which kept alive the corporate sense. They saw to it that the faith community always knew whose it was and who it is. And that was important. The church needed such a pastoral office which centered on what we might call the ministry of identity.

All well and good. But salvation, as we have noted, is also doing. The church must live. The work of Christ's atonement continues. Therefore there must also be a ministry of aliveness, of work, of vitality. This is the ministry of the laity. Not that the clergy-ministry does not bear witness, but it is the majority others (the laity) who in fact are largely in the world's arena and who therefore must put flesh and bones on the church's identity. If it is the ministry of the clergy to define the church and keep it true to itself, it is the ministry of the laity to make that church alive in this time and place, to be the hands and feet of the church body. Here then we see the close and inseparable interrelationship between the two ministries, the ministry of identity and the ministry of vitality. The balance is nicely put by Gabriel Fackre:

> The pastoral office, in whatever form, is charged with keeping alive the memories of the faith community, enabling it to know whose it is and who it is, and thereby preserving it from amnesia. It is a *ministry of identity*. . . . The *ministry of vitality* gives life and movement to the forms of the ministry of identity. The ninety-nine percent of the church that we call the laity is constituted by those vital organs and parts that enable the Body of Christ to walk and work in the world. It is the responsibility of the ministry of vitality to keep the church in motion—in mission. In this forward momentum these ministers steward the *hopes* of the church even as the ministers of vitality steward its *memories.* As the former preserves the Body from amnesia, the latter saves it from nostalgia. . . . The means of grace tended by the ministers of identity are word and sacraments . . . the means of grace stewarded by the ministers of vitality are the gifts of diakonia and koinonia by which the word takes on flesh and the Body moves. The milieu in which the ministry of identity is primarily exercised is the "church gathered," and the principal environment of the ministry of vitality is the "church scattered". . . .[1]

The ordained minister therefore is the one who promotes community (as we shall soon see) by giving identity to the localized Christ in this time and place through his or her leadership role in word, sacrament, and tradition. However, the implications of word, sacrament, and tradition are played out in the large arena where life takes place and by the people we call the laity. There is, of course, no intention of making their roles exclusive; rather it is a question of understanding and image, a question of trying to see their mutual relationship and mutual dependency. And mutual cooperation. This may take a while, and so it is to these ramifications we now turn.

2

Some have said that the whole question of lay ministries (and missions) has arisen because it was forced upon the church by declining priestly vocations. That there has been a decline is beyond doubt. Figures indicate that in 1966 this country had about 59,000 priests, both religious and secular, and 46,000 seminarians. Today, the estimate is that we have about 51,000 active priests and 16,000 seminarians, a net loss of fourteen percent of the priests and sixty-four percent of the seminarians. Sisters too, have declined in number and even more dramatically going from some 176,000 in 1968 to 129,000 in 1978. It is estimated that religious communities have lost one third of their members in the last decade. In effect, the church in America is currently struggling along with a seventeen percent permanent unemployment rate among its formerly full-time personnel. Predictions for the future are bleak. Estimates are that the church in the United States will likely have one fourth fewer priests in 1985 than in 1965. That all of this has had an influence on the emergence of lay ministries is evident, but it is not the whole picture.

To a great degree lay ministries would have emerged anyway because of many influences: from the new theology of the church and priesthood, from the explicit and implicit statements of Vatican II, from the consciousness-raising of minority groups everywhere (and in the church the laypeople could be considered that), from the emphasis on the dignity of the individual, from the insistencies of the civil rights and women's movements. In short, the material of a strong cultural distortion is here: reality is outdistancing assumptions, and old forms and the tension has forced the issue of lay ministries more effectively than any priestly vocation crisis.[2]

So the lay ministry is now here to stay but, as we indicated in the last chapter, its presence is likely to cause sensitive tensions for a long while. The ministries of identity and vitality are bound to conflict. The fundamental, on-the-spot tension is between the new role of the emerging laypeople and the role of the pastor/priest. It is flippantly easy to quote the old definitions of the various church ministers: "The pope is the servant of the servants of God. A bishop is the servant of the servant of the servants of God. A priest is the servant of the servant of the servant of the servants of God. A deacon is the servant of the servant of the servant of the servant of the servants of God. A layman is a rich man with a servant problem." It is just as easy to quickly side with the laypeople and poke fun at or heap disdain on those pastors who will not or cannot relinquish their power and authority as they conceive them. It is harder to give them the same prayerful tolerance and understanding as we would the downtrodden of society. We don't, of course, for we are all infected with the old romanticism: going to the ends of the earth to cleanse the sores of the leper while not bothering to visit our bedridden aunt in the next town. But we should make an attempt to see where the pastor is coming from—and here it is useless to disguise my own partisan feelings.

If the pastor has been a priest for twenty-years or longer then it is essential to recall his training. He was trained in the high calling and dignity of his office and rightly so; but it was essentially a calling and dignity of separateness, not that of St. Augustine's closeness. His going to a seminary, emotionally and geographically removed from society, was the first major input to his sense of holy remoteness. His limited summer jobs as a seminarian (only "fitting" ones which would not compromise his vocation or virtue) and his early special treatment added to this. At ordination and soon thereafter, his new title, celibacy, clothes and living quarters all served to keep the separateness alive and well. He was being constantly thrust to the lonely pinacle.

The expectations of the pinacle were awesome: he was to be universal leader, encyclopedic practitioner, and general specialist in everything under the sun. All by himself he was to be, in the Pauline quotes often preached to him, "all things to all men" (to which the seminary wags always added, "—and a few women"). If these pastoral expectations were high, the accountability expectations were low. As long as he did not publicly deny the Trinity his behavior, style, deportment, and policy were not under review by his superiors and certainly under no questioning by his people. His job was secure, and promotion—being made pastor—was guaranteed. All that he had to do was to breathe longer than his contemporaries. As pastor he was irremovable while his associates could come and go at his whim. Whatever daring or "unorthodox" notions he might have had were tempered by the diocesan reward system. The one who toed the mark, built buildings (not necessarily community), or who was considered bright and safe enough to hold diocesan office was rewarded. The reward usually was being made a monsignor.

Segregated from the people by training and by the system—and sometimes by temperament—the pastor was subject to the paradox that he was himself a second-class citizen in the diocesan structure. He was always subject to the chancery and its offices. He and his parish were made to serve the organization rather than the other way around. Knowing therefore that the real powers were in a chancery which incubated inbred candidates for the episcopacy who would perpetuate the system, he clung even more to his own parochial turf. Secure there, he could be indifferent to the bishop and the chancery. Their's in fact was a relationship of mutually agreed upon benign neglect. The pastor could go (and has gone) twenty or thirty years without ever having a personal visit (not official, such as at confirmation) from his bishop. Resigned to no strokes from the top, trained to no communication from the bottom, being sole pastor of sole authority became an important and essential identity factor in his life. Imagine therefore the assault on that identity when lay men and (worse) women came swinging at him with the documents of Vatican II. If someone else is going to counsel, preach, lead the prayers, read the scriptures, organize the CCD, give communion, and fill the Coke machines, what will he do all day? More to the point: who will have the real power and final decision? Who's in charge? So, emotionally trained to isolation, spiritually grounded in monasticism, conscious of no alternatives, the pastor clings all the more to his fiefdom, watching with quiet desperation, fear, or arrogance the steady erosion of his power, the democratizing of his office, and the leveling of his position. Here undoubtedly is a man who needs love, help, gentleness, and much inner and outer healing. Whatever obnoxious qualities he may show are, as John Powell reminds us, really cries of pain and appeals for help.

It is not possible to resist the temptation to ask, "Who is listening to these appeals for help?" Nor is it possible not to answer by pointing to the only persons with the old certified status and power to listen and do something: the bishops. If only they were more pastoral, giving top priority to the men in the front lines! If only they were there with many visits and affirmations and fraternal care urging renewal and legitimizing transitions to a new identity, providing opportunities for courses, making available careful sabbaticals (just recently policy in some dioceses), rerouting some into other, more compatible, work. But most bishops have been notoriously absent in the arena of the human working out of the collision of two worlds. And this is understandable too for most bishops are themselves just the super version of the pastor. Selected from top positions (some changes are being made now), they excel in administration and distance and are victimized by their offices and workload. They cannot existentially sense the dilemma or need of the pastor or, if they do, cannot themselves emotionally respond. The pastor therefore is left to clutch more violently to his role or reduced to making token gestures to the laity. The people, left without redress, give up, drop out or go elsewhere, and the bishop waits it out until death. Getting a sense of all this does not, of course, remove our anxiety if we are in a "pyramid" parish with one unshakable monarch, nasty or benign, as pastor, but it may help us to see the road he has traveled. Seeing we may have more sympathy. This may not reduce our desire to see him go but it may reduce the danger of hating the sinner along with the sin. It may even elicit prayers.

3

Still, no matter what role the pastor has the fact remains that he is a critical person in the parish, and no matter how democratic we get the leader will always set the pace, aid or hinder progress, and give overall style to the whole parochial enterprise. Think, for example, of the pontificates of Pius XII and John XXIII. The same is true in business. No matter how the votes are spread or the powers distributed the chairman of the board will give a tone. It cannot be and should not be otherwise. That is the nature of the charism of leadership.

Studies have borne out the vital role of a pastor to a congregation. A few years ago, for example, the Presbyterians did a large study as to why some parishes grow and others decline. Listed as first among some seven reasons was "strong pastoral leadership." Urban Holmes says, "All research of which I know into the life of a parish shows that the sacramental person, the priest of the community, must be clearly identifiable and responsible if that congregation is to be healthy or even to survive. . . ."[3] If therefore the pastor/priest is important and even critical to the local church then we must not dismiss him. Yet we cannot continue to tolerate one who knows only his role and identity as absolute monarch. There must be a better role and a more authentic identity that fits him in more compatibly with the theology and demands of the new church.

Two people are helpful here in plumbing the pastoral/priestly identity, other than the ministry of identity which we have already seen. One is W. Dodd who said that the ordained minister, as distinct from the nonordained one, is "the sacrament of Christ the Head in the formation of community." This fits in well with what we said in the first chapter that the church may be looked upon as a sacrament, the outward, visible sign of Jesus who in turn is the sacrament of the Father. The church is a sacramental sign and symbol of Jesus' work, presence, and grace-filled activity among mankind. It is the visible community of what living the gospel is meant to be. The ordained priest in turn is the focal sign of such a community-always-in-the-making. He is, if you will, the symbol of Jesus Gathering. The sacrament of holy orders pertains to the critical charge of rallying the community, shaping the great outward sign which we call the church, and celebrating its essential meaning in the eucharist.

Another helpful person in defining the ordained minister's role is Karl Rahner. He says this: "The priest is he who . . . preaches the Word of God by mandate of the church as a whole and therefore officially, and in such a way that he is entrusted with the highest levels of sacramental intensity of this Word." This means that all are charged with preaching and living the gospel in virtue of baptism and confirmation, but the priest is entrusted with the highest expression of this which reaches its fullest expression in the sacramental liturgies, especially the eucharist. Therefore the priest is not only a minister among others, the sign of Christ the Head who builds community, but he is also a necessary cultic figure whose presiding over the community's liturgies both reflects and heightens its identity. So, while the whole *laos* is entrusted with the saving words of Jesus, the priest, if you will, is the italicized word of what the community is speaking all the time. Bernard Cooke expresses the notion this way, "All the ministries of the ministers of the church are priestly, for the church is priestly, but the ministry of liturgical leadership bears a special relationship to the community's sacramentality and priesthood, for it exists in order to bring that priesthood to its fullest expression. It flows from the basic priesthood of the community, functions for the sake of the community priesthood, and in a sense is a specialized or intensified expression of that common priesthood."[4]

All this means that the priest's basic identity is related to the community as sign and cult. He directs its formation and presides over its being-ness and worship. It means, therefore, that he is not the whole picture but he is to *enable* the whole picture to take focus. His charism is to direct the charisms of the community. He is to enable others' ministries. In one sense he is like an orchestra leader. When Leonard Bernstein conducted the New York Philharmonic Orchestra he did not run down to play the oboe or the violin or the trumpet or the drums himself (he gave that impression sometimes); his basic job was to take some one hundred thirty people and their instruments and blend them into a harmonious whole, to make beautiful music of many talents. A conductor is in a very real sense both a community harmonizer and a cultic leader. So with the priest. As sacrament of Christ the Head, as the intensified word, he is to orchestrate community and never more powerfully than at the eucharist. He is, in Dennis Geaney's words, "a visible symbol of the unity of the Christian community. The eucharist is the central Christian symbol of community. The ordained is, therefore, the one who presides over this central act of unity. . . . Ordination is simply the recognition and public acceptance of a community member who has these gifts and willingly accepts the public role of ordained priesthood."[5]

So the pastor/priest does have an identity, not as absolute director who barks orders but as a father who builds a family. He is enabler, presider, sign, and former of community. And, with such an identity, sharing and participation are radically essential. The gifts of other people, their several ministries, their distinct voices are critical elements in community. They have these gifts by right not delegation, and it is up to the priest to rally such. Both of them together are the *laos,* each in his or her own way building up the Body of Christ. The statement of the World Council of Churches' meeting in 1961 caught the distinctions nicely: "There is an urgent need for all church members to recover the true meaning of certain words: to learn that the laity is really the 'Laos,' that is, the whole People of God in the world, including, of course, those who have been ordained; to learn that ministry means any kind of service by which a Christian exercising his peculiar skill and gift, however humble, helps his fellow Christian or his fellow men in the name of Christ. A far richer fellowship and team spirit is bound to appear as soon as the whole church comes to realize its functions as the People of God, which God himself has provided with many kinds of ministry, in which one special kind of ministry, that of the ordained clergy, is set apart to strengthen and teach, to encourage and unite all the several witnesses in their various callings whose ministry is set in the heart of the secular world."[6]

This ideal will continue to fall far short for a while. Many reasons for this are easy to come by. For one thing, there is still a real lack of theological imagination in the whole area of ministry, especially in reference to the laity. Secondly, there are still too few dioceses that have established any kind of training centers or programs for shared ministry. Thirdly, no genuine accountability system for lay ministry has been set up. This is not surprising since there scarcely exists any such accountability system for the ordained laity. Certainly neither diocesan pastoral councils or local parish councils have moved in this direction. Fourthly, viable support systems for lay ministry are generally not available yet. Fifthly, meaningful spirituality has not been divised on any large scale outside of partisan groups. Finally, official ecclesiastical legtimization for lay ministry and ordained ministry working in harmony, though here and there stated and proclaimed, is far from reality in many areas.[7] Until these areas are dealt with ministry as such will still be limited to the ordained few.

The truly creative parish may have to make its own way for a while and offer itself as a model of shared responsibility. And perhaps, when all is said and done, what we are basically talking about in the practical realm is not so much a shift of leadership away from the clergy to the laity but rather an expansion of it to include the entire community. The uncreative parish will still continue to remain one that has only one minister muting the unfulfilled charisms of others. This is the parish that is not so much a church as a bulwark, not so much a community as a service area where the people receive, watch, and silently pray. This is not what Jesus hoped for or meant when he said, "I call you no longer slaves but friends."

Notes for Chapter 6

1. Gabriel Fackre, "Ministries of Identity and Vitality," *Theology Today* 36, no. 3 (October 1979), p. 377. The whole issue on ministry is worth reading.

2. The apostolic delegate, Archbishop Jadot, addressing the bishops at their last conference (1979) said, "Let us not speak of the *raison d'etre* of the collaboration of the laity only in terms of the diminishing number of priests. The two issues, while related in the practical order, are quite distinct. . . . Every layperson, by virtue of the very gifts bestowed upon him or her, is at the same time a witness and a loving instrument of the mission of the church itself."

3. Urban Holmes, *Ministry and Imagination* (Seabury Press,

1976), p. 241. See also Loten B. Man, *New Hope for Congregations* (Seabury Press, 1972).

4. Bernard Cooke, *Ministry to Word and Sacraments* (Fortress Press, 1976), p. 641.

5. Dennis Geaney, *Emerging Lay Ministries* (Sheed, Andrews and McMeel, 1979), pp. 49–50. See also his *Full Church, Empty Rectory: Training Lay Ministers for Parishes Without Priests* (Fides/Claretian, 1980) for a discussion of some ways lay ministers are preparing themselves.

6. The New Delhi Report, 1962, p. 88. Quoted in Robert J. Hater, *The Ministry Explosion* (W. C. Brown, 1979).

7. Suggestions from Gabriel Fackre's article. See note 1. See also Mary C. Boys, SNJM, "Ministry and Education," *The Living Light* 16, no. 3 (Fall 1979), pp. 313 ff.

7. Male and Female S/He Made Them

1

When we speak of shared responsibility and a variety of ministries it is still necessary to mention in the next breath the role of women. The reason for this is the obvious and long standing second-class citizenship of women both in society and in the church. The practical subjugation of women is woven into the very consciousness of our civilization. Women as women have been long excluded from public responsibility and participation in society as a whole. Its roots go deeply into biology and anthropology, a patriarchal society and a theological dualism.[1] But whatever the causes, the fact is that in our day we have come to recognize the dignity of each individual and that any form of discrimination, whether racism or sexism, is not in accord with the gospel. So, as part of the *laos* women have moved considerably into the forefront in recent years in the church, which is as it should be. After all, women were an obvious part of Jesus' ministry, and they figured in the ministry of St. Paul. They possessed the charism of prophecy, and in the early centuries functioned as deaconesses, caring for sick women, and assisting them at baptism. At one time they even welcomed women at the doors of the church. Gradually, along with men, they were reduced to passive laity but, unlike men, were officially and emotionally excluded from church participation. Only recently has their potential been recognized and tapped. They are now engaged in all kinds of missions and ministries. Their rightful place is reflected in all kinds of documents such as the one entitled, "As One Who Serves: Reflections on the Pastoral Ministry of Priests in the United States" which says, "In the light of the priests' tasks to hold the community accountable to its self-identity and to call forth leadership, the priest can be expected to exercise some real responsibility in regard to the complex question of the developing role of women in the context of the total church's mission and ministry. . . . It is essential for the life and mission of the church that priests encourage women in responding to the call to assume more influential and responsible positions of leadership and service in the church and society. Priests have a serious responsibility to help ensure that decision-making processes at parish, diocesan, and national levels incorporate the voices and insights of women." Women, therefore, are now on parish councils, involved as CCD teachers, and function as lectors, cantors, and eucharistic ministers. Others, especially sisters, are heavily involved in pastoral ministries from being chancellor of dioceses as in the diocese of Lafayette, Louisiana, associate pastors (as in my own parish) to pastors of parishes such as found in South America and Europe and even one or two places in this country. There is obviously a long way to go, but the forces of shared ministry are at work and women in the future will be an intregal part of it all.

Someone, of course, is going to bring up the question of women priests, and I am not courageous nor certain enough myself to settle it (except with certain personal postures), even though the church has given its answer for the time being. There are good arguments on both sides and, at this writing, I am not focused sufficiently on the theological issues to know for certain the answer. We must content ourselves to reviewing the arguments which the Congregation for the Doctrine of the Faith gave in a declaration published on January 27, 1977 when it affirmed that it "judged it necessary to recall that the church, in fidelity to the example of the Lord, does not consider herself authorized to admit women to priestly ordination." (The convoluted language here is a hint that things aren't as settled as they seem.)

First of all, as an introduction, the whole question is not terribly new as a burning issue. It goes back only a few decades and it was kicked off in 1958 when the Swedish Lutheran Church decided to admit women to the pastoral office. Here was a novelty that caused much speculation. From here the admitting of women to the pastoral office spread to the Reformed churches of France, but a whole new interest arose when in 1971 and in 1973 the Anglican bishop of Hong Kong ordained three women. Then in July of 1974 in Philadelphia eleven women were ordained in the Episcopal church (afterwards declared invalid by the House of Bishops). Later, in June of 1975, the Anglican Church in Canada approved in principle the ordination of women to the priesthood, and this was confirmed by the General Synod of the Church of England. Such were the events, stirred by the feminist movement, which brought the question of the ordination of women pressingly into the Roman Catholic camp.

Getting back to the Catholic church declaration which felt that it does not consider itself authorized to admit women to priestly ordination, three main lines of arguments are used (and it might be worth studying them if only in order to refute them). First and most critically there is the basic question of Jesus' will here. After all, women were not only so obviously a part of his ministry but he treated them so very differently from the custom of his time. His culture put women in a very inferior position. Was not the traditional Jewish prayer that one thanked God for "not being a slave, a Gentile, or a woman"? But Jesus broke this mold. He was a maverick who broke so many Jewish laws and customs. For example, against the tide of the times, he associated with tax collectors and ate with them (Lk 15:1–2), healed on the Sabbath (Mk 3:2), opposed the established religion (Mt 23:1–36), and rejected ritual taboos (Mk 7:1–23). But the point is: If Jesus favored women and was not above rejecting so much in his culture, why did he not go all the way and make them part of the Twelve and give them the priesthood? Obviously, it is concluded, he did not want to.

Even more. Jesus taught things far more startling and far more outrageous to the times than any priesthood of women. He taught three persons in One God. He taught that he, as a man was God. He taught that bread and wine became his body and blood. At least the first church took and interpreted such teachings and they have remained a steadfast tradition in the face of all kinds of schisms, heresies, and persecutions. What could really be more shocking than these concepts? If therefore (so the argument goes), Jesus went against so many customs and so alienated the people of his times with his claims to being God to the extent that they killed him for it (Jn 19) and with his promise to give his body and blood as food and drink that many left him for saying it (Jn 6:66), then why did he not do a far lesser thing and give women the priesthood—at least, one would think, his mother Mary? Again, the answer seems to be that this was not his will.

Still, there was time for change when Christianity moved

to the Greek and Roman worlds of Athens, Alexandria, and Rome where priestesses abounded and female goddesses were common. Why did not a St. Paul, for example, extend the priesthood to women as he did to men? After all, he was the one who declared in words often quoted by pro-women's ordination today, "For as many of you as were baptized into Christ have put on Christ. There is neither Jew nor Greek, there is neither slave or free, there is neither male or female; for you are all one in Christ Jesus" (Gal 3:27–28). Paul apparently felt that absolute equality in baptismal life is quite a different thing from the structure of the ordained ministry since he did not follow through on his words and ordain women. Could it be, again, that in his conduct he was following the will of Christ? Yes, there is Paul's dictum that "women should keep silence in churches" for they are not permitted to speak (1 Cor 14:34) and his words, "I do not allow a woman to teach or to exercise authority over men" (1 Tim 2:11–14), but these sayings may not be authentic. There are in fact many authentic ones that do reflect his thought such as "the head of the woman is the man" (1 Cor 11:3), words which he apparently thinks are compatible with "all are one in Christ Jesus." Anyway, the intent of Jesus and his apostolic witnesses seems to be clear: it is not the divine will to ordain women for when they both had a chance to move on this issue they did not.

Secondly, there is the undisputed fact that in both traditions of East and West, from the very beginning up to the present day, in an unbroken line, women have never been made priests. This is somewhat noteworthy since the East has often broken with the West on important issues. Women were deacons and were in fact ordained as such, but even here their functions were far less extensive and less important than their male colleagues. Their tasks as deacons seemed confined to assisting in the baptism of women for reasons of decency, but they themselves were not permitted to baptize. They have never been priests or bishops. We do read of lady abbesses in the Middle Ages—whose numbers were far less than the romantic novels would have us believe—and they did have power associated with bishops. Here, however, there is the technical distinction between office and jurisdiction. Usually both are found together in the same person: a man is ordained a bishop and automatically has jurisdiction over a certain territory. But it is possible to separate these usually joined powers, and this is what happened in the case of the lady abbesses. They appointed clergy to their posts and granted them faculties. In a word, they had the power of jurisdiction but never the power of sacred orders that allowed them to, say, celebrate the eucharist or ordain. So the tradition has remained intact from the very first: women were not ordained to the priesthood. This joined with the example of Christ and the apostles leads the present declaration to think that such is God's will. (We have prescinded from the medieval prejudices about the inferiority of women making them ineligible for ordination, for beneath such chauvinism, there were root questions all along as well, especially the theological ones we will explore now.)

Finally, there are questions of what we might call "fittingness" that a priest should be male and the more esoteric question of sacramental symbolism. The fittingness argument, as Michael Novak puts it, comes from the natural arrogance of man. He is the one more full of pride and attached to power. Were he therefore to preach and celebrate a gospel of submission, humility, and love it would be more powerful. "A woman preaching humility, meekness, and service would not have been a scandal to the world. The gospel would have had a very different symbolism embodied in a woman . . . the male is the more scandalizing and telling symbol of Christianity. The male is not the better, or truer Christian, but he is, alas, the more surprising witness. When the 'oppressed' preach humility, the message is not as clear."[2]

Aligned with this concept is the theological question of sacramental symbolism which says that "in the actions that call for the character of ordination, for the community (the priest) is—with all the effectiveness proper to the sacraments—the image and symbol of Christ himself who calls, forgives, and accomplishes the sacrifice of the covenant." The point is that a sacramental sign must have content and must be rooted in proportion and reality. Christ is the actor and agent in the eucharist and the forgiveness of sin. One who acts in his name and in his person, therefore, ought to have, or better, to be, a correlative sign system. In short, a male is the commensurate symbol of the male Christ. This is due, of course, not of any inherent virtue in males as over and against females, but out of God's freedom to utter the message the way he chooses to utter it through a male messiah. The official commentary on the declaration puts it this way:

> The declaration therefore suggests that it is by analyzing the nature of order and its character that we will find the explanation for the exclusive call of men to the priesthood and episcopate. This analysis can be outlined in three propositions: 1) in administering the sacraments that demand the character of ordination the priest does not act in his own name, but in the person of Christ; 2) this formula, as understood by tradition, implies that the priest is a sign in the sense in which this term is understood in sacramental theology; 3) it is precisely because the priest is a sign of Christ the savior that he must be a man and not a woman. . . . It

> would not accord with "natural resemblance," with that obvious "meaningfulness," if the memorial of the supper were to be carried out by a woman; for it is not just the recitation involving the gestures and words of Christ, but an action, and the sign is efficacious because Christ is present in the minister who consecrates the eucharist (and so the male minister must be an apt sign for the male Christ). . . . The difference between the sexes is something willed by God from the beginning, according to the account in Genesis and is directed both to communion between persons and to the begetting of human beings. And it must be affirmed first and foremost that the fact that Christ is a man and not a woman is neither incidental nor unimportant in relation to the economy of salvation. In what sense? Not of course, in the material sense, as has sometimes been suggested . . . but because the whole economy of salvation has been revealed to us through the essential symbols from which it cannot be separated, and without which we would be unable to understand God's design.

The "essential symbol" is the male Christ: hence the male priest.

2

It is clear that not everyone will agree with the official declaration described in these last pages. Scripture scholar John Donahue, for example, says we ought not to make too much over Jesus' being a maverick. He indeed did depart from some norms but in other ways he was traditional. He attended the synagogue (Lk 4:16), prayed before meals (Mk 6:41), wore ritual fringes on his garment (Mt. 9:20), invoked the teaching of Moses (Mk 10:28–31) and followed the Passover prescriptions (Mk 14:12–31).[3] While unorthodox in some matters, maybe his choice of men only belongs to his orthodox side. Also, there is an interesting speculation about who presided at the first eucharist. The apostles were in Jerusalem, but who did it elsewhere? St. Paul lists among community charisms apostles and, secondly, prophets. In the *Didache,* prophets were proving troublesome (as we have already seen), but the author lets them preside at the eucharist even though he wishes to have this job handed over to the presbyters and deacons—which eventually it was. What is of note is that there is no doubt whatsoever that prophets also included female ones. Did they then preside at the eucharist?

Not only does St. Paul speak of many charisms of varying degress of importance for the building up of the Body of Christ (Eph 4:11; 1 Cor 12:28; Rom 12:4–8) but also the New Testament evidence in no way indicates that one group controlled or exercised them all. Rather such responsibility was shared by various groups, including women. Furthermore, according to Paul, the requirements for apostleship were to have seen the Risen Lord and to have received from him the commission to proclaim the gospel. Women fulfill both requirements. They were the first to discover the empty tomb and, according to some traditions, the first to see the Risen Christ, and they were designated by Christ as his witnesses (Lk 24:48). According to Luke the requirement for apostleship was to have accompanied Jesus in his earthly ministry. Women obviously fill this criterion. Women were a part of the first church (Acts 1:14–15) and received the Pentecostal Spirit. They were instrumental in founding churches (Acts 18:2), were in leadership roles (Rom 16:1; Phil 4:2–3) and functioned in public worship (1 Cor 1:5). They taught converts (Acts 18:26) and were prophets (1 Cor 11:5). The final greeting of Paul in his epistle to the Romans mentions a woman minister, Phoebe (Rom 16:1), and possibly a woman apostle, Junia (Rom 16:7). Note that all these functions are what we would call priestly ministries. And as for Jesus' silence about women, the only accurate remark to make is that he gave no clear and positive norm. We know that there were no women among the Twelve. On the other hand, there were no Gentiles, slaves, or Samaritans either, male or female.

It would seem, therefore, that all that we can say about the New Testament evidence is contained in the summary report of the committee on the role of women in early christianity appointed by the executive board of the Catholic Biblical Association of America:

An examination of the biblical evidence shows the following:

> that there is positive evidence in the NT that ministries were shared by various groups and that women did in fact exercise roles and functions later associated with priestly ministry; that the arguments against the admission of women to priestly ministry based on the praxis of Jesus and the apostles, disciplinary regulations, and the created order cannot be sustained. The conclusions we draw, then, is that the NT evidence, while not decisive by itself, points towards the admission of women to priestly ministry.[4]

As far as early tradition goes, Roger Gryson in conclusion to his book *The Ministry of Women in the Early Church* says, "Therefore, one may ask once more whether the Fathers, sharing in a civilization which accorded women little place in the exercise of public duties, could envision with sufficient freedom of spirit the possibility of admitting women to a priestly ministry. There are reasons why, in the eyes of many, the scriptural argument, as well as the traditional one, in the present state of elaboration, are not sufficient to invalidate the issue of women priests and require, instead, to be put to good scholarly use to solve the prejudiced issues implicit in them."[5] Another writer comments:

> . . . To exclude women from access to the ministry amounts to legalizing a charism. It means making a law according to which it is decided that human beings, because of their sex, and therefore because of a natural condition, are excluded a priori from the ministry of the priesthood. Whether one likes it or not, the natural condition is itself the condition of the charism. Here it is not a case of the charism exploding the institutional but of the institutional restricting the charism. To refer to the will of Jesus when he never expressed it is not enough to justify the kind of relation put forward here between the charism and what has been instituted. All the precautions taken to make it clear that this is not a question of assuming that the male is superior to the female do not change the exclusive bending of a gratuitousness which is turned into a preference of nature. As to the explanations which point out that Jesus was a male and that therefore only males can symbolize the presidency of the eucharist, this amounts to saying that in the ministry the natural condition is more important than the breath of the Spirit which precisely breaks down all the barriers imprisoning men and women, all created in the likeness of God.[6]

The Catholic Theological Society Task Force of June 7, 1978 listed eleven reasons why women should be ordained:

1. It is unjust to exclude women from pastoral office when this office is denied to them as a class and on principle without regard to their personal qualifications.

2. The demands of mission and the needs of church require that any competent person (man or woman) be eligible for pastoral office.
3. Through baptism, all Christians participate in the priesthood of the faithful. All should likewise be eligible to test their vocation for pastoral office.
4. Many women experience a desire to serve in capacities of spiritual leadership and sacramental service. . . . They look upon their attraction to this work as a call from the Spirit.
5. There is a growing consensus among Anglican and Protestant churches in favor of the ordination of women.
6. The official ministry of the church should represent the variety of persons to whom the church ministers.
7. Ordination of women would prevent further alienation of modern women from the church.
8. The mutability of tradition in other areas of church life . . . provides a precedent for change in this one.
9. Women have a special experience of life to bring to the ministry.
10. It is time to actualize the full implications of Galatians 3:28.
11. The ancient tradition of the church provides a liturgy of ordination of deaconesses for women, and this gives precedent for their ordination to the priesthood.

Some of these eleven arguments do not appear particularly strong taken separately. Perhaps more effective is the background we saw previously: that all the *laos,* the people of God, in the words of Vatican II, share in the priestly prophetic and kingly role of Jesus. Therefore, women, as members of that *laos* already possess the priesthood which for all is one grounded in service and obedience—a notion that impelled scripture scholar Raymond Brown to remark that "in terms of the priesthood of all believers, Mary, the mother of Christ, is the greatest of priests." What we call the clerical state within that priesthood grew up, as we have seen, more as an institutional necessity for order and stability, reflecting pretty much the normal political structures of society. Therefore the ordained clergy rightly deal with the public forum; the state is an expression of officialdom. Therefore, a woman who seeks ordination is not basically seeking the priesthood for she already possesses that: what she is seeking is her place in the officialdom of the church. This includes all that we have seen: the sacramental status of leadership, sign, and cult and entry into recognized status and into the decision making processes of the church. Looked at this way, then, when we ask whether women are ordainable we are really asking, in the words of Edward Foye, "first, whether woman, any woman, is capable of maturity, of the fullness of humanity. . . . The second is whether we are ready to allow the Spirit of God to breathe where it will (Jn 3:8); or will we continue to quench the Spirit (1 Thess 5:19)?" This is the real question that the Christian community has to grapple with. And the answer would seem obvious.

Also, looked at this way the question for any woman aspiring to ordination these days becomes significant and challenging in that she must consider this: there are genuine if irregular signs that the church is on its way to full reformation in which eventually the decision-making processes will in fact move out of the closed male episcopacy into the wider community. If this is so, any woman candidate for ordination must ponder if she really wants to have current membership in the present male-dominated clerical system which may be slowly unraveling anyway; or could she work for an all out reform of the church in her present priesthood of the *laos?* The answer is hers to make. Meanwhile the overriding consideration to keep in mind is that the essence of the priesthood is service not power. The where and how of such service has to be pondered by each person, man or woman.

When all is said and done there is the gut feeling that the women's ordination issue will not really be settled on the basis of the New Testament practice or indications alone; nor will the issue be settled on speculation and theory alone. It will arise from the community's practice. That's why it is pastorally needed to give women as full a place in the community and eucharistic celebrations as possible: women lectors, cantors, altar servers, gift bearers, not to mention women theologians, associate pastors, and chancellors. It will be this collective practice and witnessing which will lead to a more fruitful dialogue. Meanwhile, as the debate goes on, it should not blind us to the larger indisputable fact: that women have a rightful place in mission and ministry and any parish that does not use them with their various charisms to full potential is not only slowing down the discussion, not only slowing the community's growth but also distorting the church's image as truly catholic.[7]

3

We have spent a long time on this first foundation of the creative parish because ministry is so new on the current scene. Nor have we said the last word, for ministry is still an unfinished business: even its very definition is far from settled. We can quickly end our discussion, then with some final observations. We should take note, for example, that the whole novel issue of lay ministry today is part and parcel of a typical revivalist "distortion." It represents a decided shift away from an almost exclusive focus on the child and the school to the parish and to an adult-centered church.

This new interest in lay ministry may also reveal a mild form of anticlericalism as, true to its revivalist coloring, it is democratic enough to include women and all lay people in the running of the church. Lay ministry will certainly play a part in the restructuring of the Catholic parish along the principles of shared responsibility and discipleship. Bishop Albert Ottenweller, remarking how everything funnels down to the pastor's desk, understands why the pastor cannot handle the volume and therefore why so many programs do not work. He suggests structural change in this way: "One way to think of structuring a staff organization is with the pastor at the center, relating to four to six others, and you keep on going down further from the center. If that is done and the lines of communication and authority are clearly delineated, it is possible to take on as many apostolates as the parish wants. But if the pastor is at the top by himself, he is going to be relating to every parishioner, and it is likely that everybody will come to the pastor. This is not the kind of structure that gives dignity to people as it should. This is one of the difficulties in parish reconstruction—for the pastor to be willing to share the power."

We may note too that this whole lay ministry movement can be susceptible to revivalism's traditional turning inward and its tendency to fundamentalism. Likewise, the whole movement, at least in its current form, seems to be attracting many more women than men, both lay and religious. They are the ones heavily enrolled in the various schools which give out pastoral ministry degrees. As we shall mention again at the end of the book, the women are the ones getting theologically and spiritually sophisticated, leaving their busy and traveling husbands behind. The net result, from a pastoral point of view, may be to aggravate family communication and unity. Again, perhaps a restructuring of parish schedules and a real effort to attract the men can keep the groundswell of lay ministry on a balanced footing. In any case, we may still rightfully see the emergence of the lay ministry, no matter what the cautions, as a critical element in the restoration of the church in a new age. Lay ministry may well be the chief strength of a church about to confront the twenty-first century. Certainly it will be the best ally of the creative parish.

Notes for Chapter 7

1. One writer offers this theory: "During the Late Bronze Age, wars, famines, and plagues created a demographic crisis which intensified the role of women in domestic affairs and childbearing. When the crisis passed, the restriction of women to domestic circles was ingrained in Israelitic society and ultimately became the basis for their subordination through the remainder of the biblical period and on into modern times" Carol Meyers, ("The Roots of Restriction: Women in Early Israel," *Biblical Archaeologist* 41, no. 3 [September, 1978], p. 91ff.).

2. Michael Novak, *Commonweal* (September 2, 1977), p. 563ff.

3. John Donahue, *America* 136, no. 13 (April 2, 1977), p. 286.

4. *Catholic Biblical Quarterly* 41, no. 4 (October 1979), p. 612. For a reprint of the entire statement, write to *Catholic Biblical Quarterly,* The Catholic University of America, Washington, D.C. 20064. Enclose 25¢ $5.00 for 25 copies.

5. Roger Gryson, *The Ministry of Women in the Early Church* (Liturgical Press, 1976), p. 114.

6. Christian Dubuoc, "Charism as the Social Expression of the Unpredictable Nature of Grace," in *Concilium* 109 (Seabury Press, 1978), p. 95.

7. There is a unique diocesan effort in Canada dedicated solely to fostering women's ministries. It provides training leading to the receiving of a diocesan mandate. For information write Rev. A. McMillan, Good Shepherd Church, P.O. Box 610, Espanola, Ontario POP 1Co, Canada.

8. Spirituality and Scope

1

People are always giving compliments that hurt. After a good homily at a wedding, for instance, they will come up to the preacher and exclaim, "You must be encountered!" and when he says no he hasn't, they appear not only disappointed but slightly scandalized that a charism could be found outside their movement. And the preacher is left with the slightly deflated feeling that somehow his questioners have silently uttered an incantation that canceled out the compliment. Or if a priest transmits to them some spark of enthusiasm they say, oh, you are charismatic and when he protests that he is not they insist behind his back that he is but he doesn't know it. Again, the preacher or the priest is left to feel that their own little world of gift and prophecy is small potatoes indeed and is nothing if not latched onto a current movement.

Something of the same feeling comes to the progressive pastor when sincere people remark what an active parish he has. Yes, it is active, but he wonders, "Do I really want to be known primarily for that? Does my parish really want that reputation?" He knows what the people mean who make the compliment and he accepts it graciously, but he feels let down. Somehow (he apologizes to the Lord) he has not got the message across that the heart and soul of the parish is not activity as such, gratifying as it may be, but spirituality. By this he means that the parish, through its very presence and through its activities somehow must project the Risen Jesus and provide space, time, and place for marvelous encounters with him. The health of the parish is measured not only by works but by faith as well. He wishes people would remark instead, "We sense the presence of the Lord, a certain Spirit, in your parish."

Spirituality, which is our second foundation of the creative parish, embraces the collective understanding of the people as to who they are and what they are essentially about. It refers to the collective sense they have of Jesus and his gospel. It refers to a sense of mission which they have acquired through prayer and reflection. Or, to put it another way, in its most fundamental sense parish spirituality deals with the relationship between contemplation and ministry. It tries to come to terms with both. It tries (or should try) to work out the answer Henri Nouwen gives: "To contemplate is to *see* and to minister is to make visible. . . . .The contemplative life is a life with a vision and the life of ministry is the life in which this vision is revealed to others."[1] The uncreative parish is not even aware of the tension between contemplation and ministry. It tends to lean to one side or the other: it exists either with such passivity and quietude that it appears like a misplaced monastery offering gnostic graces to perservering mystics or with such active motion that no one can pause long enough in the running to see where he or she is running to.

American Catholics, by their very heritage, are success and activity oriented. The active parish *is* considered a sign of vitality—which may be perfectly true. On the other hand, such a parish may be hiding some very real spiritual shallowness. Parishes, like individuals, can effectively run away from God through religion, through "being busy about many things." Only one thing is necessary but few parishes seem to choose "the better part," at least consistently.

It is this ambivalence which brought forth from Father George Maloney these remarks: "What is lacking in our American, Western parishes is the sense of mystery going into liturgy and not just seeing it as a problem to be solved: how to have a better microphone system, take collections, have the lectors there on time and prepared. That's all necessary, but we need to push these people into the spiritual persons who then know why they teach CCD, why they're on the social committee, why they're giving expertise to running the finances of the parish. I think the lay people have emerged in the sense of 'doing' in the parish, but they haven't emerged in the sense of 'being' through deeper prayer. And I think most pastors are not on that level. They're still organizers, running a parish that has problems and they must seek the answers. Until they all reach that level, you're not going to have an emerging lay person exemplified by his or her sense of prayer. The whole parish must be a praying parish. The pastor, the nuns, the lay people."[2] These words sum up the challenge of parish spirituality.

Actually, the irony in all of this "doing" and not "being" is that people are really hungering for God more than ever before, and unanchored activity simply does not feed them. Our young people, as we know, are leaving in droves, not because we are not providing sports programs, but because they cannot sense the presence of a caring Jesus. They turn to the cults, as we have seen, to give a poverty, chastity, and obedience they would not render their traditional church. They seek mystical experiences because they have never heard about prayer—not academically but in their fellow parishioners and clergy. They read, in Eastern garb, John of the Cross or Teresa of Avila not knowing that these Spanish mystics belong to their heritage. They join fundamentalist Jesus movements and pour daily over their New Testaments because it is new to them even after twenty years in their Catholic parish. They seek, look for and need the intimacy and support of a small affirming group which many large, impersonal parishes do not and cannot afford. They are forever being taught but never listened to; stuffed with information, deprived of formation. How many young people or adults can speak movingly, deeply, and affectionately about their parishes and what they found there? There is no doubt that the parish has to come to terms with its spirituality, its gospel identity, its contemplative spirit. The needs are many:

> You do not have to be a great prophet to say that coming decades will most likely see not only more wars, more hunger, and more oppression, but also desperate attempts to escape them all. We have to be prepared for a period in which suicide will be as widespread as drugs are now, in which new types of flagellants will roam the country frightening the people with the announcement of the end of all things, and in which many new exotic cults with intricate rituals will try to ward off a final catastrophe. We have to be prepared for an outburst of new religious movements using Christ's name for the most un-Christian practices. In short, we have to be prepared to live in a world in which fear, suspicion, mutual distrust, hatred, physical and mental torture, and in increasing confusion will darken the hearts of millions of people.
>
> It is in the midst of this dark world that the Christian community is being tested. Can we be light, salt, and leaven to our brothers and sisters in the human family? Can we offer

> hope, courage, and confidence to the people of this era? Can we break through the paralyzing fear by making those who watch us exclaim, "See how they love each other, how they serve their neighbor, and how they pray to their Lord?"[3]

Facing such questions should not hinder us from reveling in the deserved glory in being an active parish. Certainly activity is to be preferred to the pious coma (Frank Sheed's phrase) of some parishes. The challenge of spirituality, however, is that the parish, like Jesus, must commute between the plains and the mountains in order to test its witness and its sacramental sign. This is most necessary for we shall not convince ourselves or others of the cause of Christ unless we are more spiritually alive than the rest of the world. We need an unmistakable parish spirituality to infuse our progress and activity with the Spirit. We need it simply to prevent ourselves from becoming a noisy gong and a clanging cymbal.

2

To do this is not an easy task, but there are some suggestions that can help greatly. First of all, the parish staff must be convinced of the necessity of a "praying parish." That's where it usually begins, where the tone is set. And there is no more effective way to bring this about than for the staff itself to program several days away each year for prayer, sharing, and reflection. This staff means not merely the clergy and religious, but those active lay ministers in the parish as well. Away from the parish in shared prayer the staff must continually evaluate the parish in relation to the gospel. It has to ask questions and be ready for certain reforms. It has to see where it has been led astray and where various successes might have distracted it from the Lordship of Jesus. The staff itself must therefore be the first to look, discern, share, and pray and build up a sense of Christian community among its own members. It is not too much to say that its ability to share and pray together is a reliable indicator of general parish vitality and spirituality. Moreover, the question here is not only the staff's collective sense of wholeness and truth, but also each individual member's relationship to the Lord as well. Each one must be confronted by the haunting words of Charles Davis:

> They come to talks by speakers like myself. They hear about the new liturgy, about the new understanding of the layman's role, about collegiality, about the church and the world, about a thousand and one new and exciting ideas. They are duly impressed. But who will speak to them quite simply about God, as of a Person he intimately knows and make the reality and presence of God come alive for them once more?
>
> Before such need, how superficial, pathetically superficial, is much of the busyness of renewal. We reformers know so much about religion and about the church and about theology, but we stand empty-handed and uncomfortable when confronted with the sheer hunger for God. Holiness is less easily acquired than fluency in contemporary thinking. But people who after listening to our enthusiastic discourses, quietly ask us to lead them to God are, though they do not know it, demanding holiness in us.
>
> I fear they may find everything else but that. The harnessing of modern publicity and know-how to reforming zeal is a potent cause of deception. Saints were required in the past to renew the church. We suppose we can get by as spiritual operators.
>
> It has long been recognized that religion may be used as way of escaping God. People carry out their formal religious duties punctiliously, because this allows them to leave God out

> of the rest of their lives. Zeal for renewal may be used in the same way. The busier we are about liturgical matters, the lay apostolate, ecumenism, the biblical renewal, reformation of church structures, and all the rest, the more incessant our activities in the cause of *aggiornamento,* the less need there is to confront the reality of God in our own lives. We are covering over the void in our own hearts. A fear prevents us from admitting the emptiness we should find there.[4]

Secondly, the parish must develop strong lay leadership. Lay ministers should be encouraged not only to acquire the professional and academic expertise they need to perform well, but also to cultivate the spirit of prayer and contemplation. Otherwise they might fall into that fearful category of what someone has termed, "theologians who do not pray." How serious the parish is about this is always defined by where it puts its money. It should send such lay ministers away for directed retreats and spiritual direction for their own sakes as well as to learn how to train others in these arts. Along this line the parish should not neglect to cultivate its live-in contemplatives: the elderly and house bound.

Years ago a national magazine had as its promotional motto, "Never Underestimate the Power of a Woman." A variation of this gives us the third suggestion for developing parish spirituality, namely, never underestimate the power of the liturgy. Because the weekend liturgy by its very definition is public and has the most people present, it can speak more about our spiritual value system than most anything else in the parish. In practice, this means not only that the liturgy should be well done, but, more to our purposes here, it should be free of distraction—even worthwhile ones. Otherwise the messages keep getting mixed, the images conflict. Either people are there totally dedicated to the prayerful worship of the Father through their brother Jesus or not. Not that this has to be so rigid as to evoke some old Puritan earnestness that kills all aspects of human and parish life. Rather it means that unfitting distractions should not overlay the main purpose of what the parish is about when it meets to pray publicly. For example, there should be no buying and selling before and after Mass as a general practice no matter how lovely the cause. Other creative ways can be found of doing this sort of thing. People should not always be meeting benign vendors on their way in or out waving chances in their faces for the latest color TV or car—especially if the scripture readings for that particular weekend have been prophetically disturbing about our many commercial idols, or the *anawim* of the Old Testament who are Boat People of today.

The people have come to church for one purpose: to find together in their fractured week perhaps the one time and place where publicly and without embarrassment or hostility they can profess that Jesus Christ is Lord. They have come to hear a good homily which should not be dissipated by parish merchants as soon as they exit. They have come to find support for their Christian value system and family life which have been subtly attacked all week long. Here is the one place where, without apology and patronization, they can be a collective witness to the gospel. Here is the one place where wealth and position ultimately do not count for they have attended the funerals of the most affluent parishioners. Here is the one place they look for affirmation, support, encouragement, and community. They simply should not be consistently seduced by unexamined distractions. It follows likewise that bulletin announcements should never be read to a literate congregation if they receive a printed one after Mass (never before, lest we give them reading material), and only one collection should ever be taken up regardless of all kinds of diocesan mandates and appeals. A little foresight can work out a system whereby such extras can be foreseen and little by little provided for. Once more, it is not a question of people being nickled and dimed to death during Mass. It is a question of giving space to the Lord with as few interruptions as possible. It is a question of not underestimating the power of an integral, well-done liturgy to promote the spirituality of the parish.

Fourthly, the parish should draw on the spiritual gifts of the people. Pastors are not hesitant to ask for parishioners' material assistance and vocational expertise, but how many ask for and promote their spiritual gifts? There are more avenues for them here than we think. There is no reason, for example, why, on an appropriate occasion, some lay person could not speak from the pulpit. We often have "witness night" for our confirmation children so it is not unnatural to have someone, on a special occasion, to bear to others his or her witness to the gospel. Families can take turns being ministers and servers at the parish High Mass and they can prepare, conduct, and lead the Stations of the Cross on the Fridays of Lent with a meditation homily at the end. Individuals can be asked to write seasonal meditations as a Sunday bulletin insert.

There is no rule, either, that says that *every* morning forever and ever we must have daily Mass. People are so Mass-conscious that every occasion from winning the ball game to kicking off the parish carnival must have its Mass. The poverty of such a situation is evident when we realize that there are two other elements to the public liturgy of the church: the sacraments and the divine office. Why not, on one morning of the week, have the office? Laypeople can conduct it and the eucharistic minister can distribute communion as part of the service as well as preach in the sense of sharing ideas on the scripture reading.

Even at daily Mass, the dialogue homily might encourage the verbalizing of some truly profound thoughts that the laity have but seldom have a public chance to share. A parish could promote a "prayer-pal" system for Advent and Lent. The names of all the parishioners are put in a box in front of the altar and people take one out at random. This is their secret prayer pal for whom they shall pray all season. They initially send a little card telling the other of this fact and sign it "Your Secret Prayer Pal." After the season is over, they reveal themselves by having their pal over for coffee and cake. This not only builds community by introducing people who otherwise might not know each other, but it helps them to meet in the essential fellowship of prayer.

These things, plus parish prayer groups and bible study groups, are not merely gimmicks. They are vivid indications to all of where the parish's priorities are and that spirituality is not only the gift of the leadership but is the charism of the whole People of God.

A final suggestion concerns parish councils. This is not the place to go into them here; but it is the place to briefly point out how they, above all, can promote parish spirituality and serve as a model. Too many parish councils are spinning on the wrong axis: they are democratic groups of well-meaning people wrestling with the material aspects of the parish plant. Much energy goes into distributing the budget and worrying about janitors, salaries, roof leaks and the mechanics of running the parish efficiently. While there is nothing wrong in this and such agendas are quite necessary, the parish council should not project *only* these concerns. There should be some arrangement whereby the voting members of the council have as their basic mandate prayer and discernment. Others with vested interests may ask, appeal, and seek their needs, but some core group on the council must take time for the Spirit. Some core people must be there to ask the right questions and to have an overall spiritual view of what the parish is and where it is going. Someone, in short, must be tapped into the spiritual vision of the church. That is why mere good will for members is not enough. They should all be required to go through a period of training and shared prayer. They must not only be familiar with the documents of Vatican II but also with the bible. Spiritual discernment must absolutely be a priority, and time spent in prayer must not be considered a luxury holding up the "business" of the council, but its essential pivot.[5]

Spirituality is truly an essential second foundation for the creative parish. Unfortunately, the uncreative parish, as we indicated before, does not even raise the issue, for it feels that it can go along on what has been handed onto it from generations before. Yet, without a spiritual vision, frequently reexamined, such parishes more easily fall into the philosophy of bigger and better. They tend to multiply activities which, in view of the gospel often become a costly extravagance. One thinks here of Thoreau's remarks about his house. He said, "I had three chairs in my house: one for solitude, two for friendship, three for society. When visitors came in larger and unexpected numbers there was but the third chair for them all, but they generally economized by standing up. It is surprising how many great men and women a small house will contain. . . . Many of our houses, both public and private, with their almost innumerable apartments, their huge halls and their cellars for the storage of wines and other munitions of peace, appear to me extravagantly large for their inhabitants."

Some parishes are like that: too many chairs, attractive and varied, with the one for solitude and prayer left too often unused.

3

When we come to talk about the third foundation of the creative parish we are basically speaking about its ministry of healing and reconciliation. We are talking about parish scope, the width of its collective Christ-like embrace. The uncreative parish has a rather narrow scope, namely, standard provisions for traditional people in the Rosary, Altar, and Holy Name societies, and the Catholic Daughters of America. For their spiritual needs there are the standard services such as novenas, missions, and communion breakfasts. While these organizations and devotions are surely worthwhile, their existence as a parish monopoly indicates that such a parish has no awareness that times have changed, that people and structures are different from what they used to be, and that the social scene has radically altered. There is no sense that we are engaged in a current revival. There is no awareness of multiplying subgroups and what they reveal, of a shrunken world and what it means, of the existence of cults and what they symbolize, or of social dislocations and what they demand. In fact, in the uncreative parish there exists strains of triumphalism and a posture of pyramidal righteousness. Such a parish continues to exist in a conventional mold, for conventional people, offering conventional outlets for conventional socializing and praying.

The trouble with this picture is that people are becoming less and less conventional, neighborhoods less and less homogenous, and living patterns less and less stable. For example, the latest official Census Bureau surveys show some changes. Our population is growing at a decreasing rate for one thing. The increase was 0.8 percent in 1978 as compared with the annual average of 1.3 percent in the 1960s and the 1.7 percent of the 1950s. People are getting older as a national average and so there is talk of "the graying of America." The median age in 1978 was just under thirty compared to twenty-eight in 1970. Senior citizens are more in evidence and in years to come will be predominant. The white population of America continues to decline while blacks, Hispanics, and other minorities increase. Adults are better educated as a whole than ever and are leaving the large metropolitan areas to live in the suburbs and elsewhere. People are postponing marriage until later and later. For example, the proportion of women twenty to twenty-four who have never married is one third larger today than ten years ago. Sadly the divorce rate continues to soar to all time records, and there has been a dramatic increase of couples living together without benefit of the contract of marriage (though not without some "palimony" papers in hand for their breakup record is not enviable). Finally, family size is smaller, and, while income is up, buying power is static.

These cold statistics tell us something about some very warm people who now make up our parishes or increasingly will. The uncreative parish will not see them or, if seeing, will not provide. Its narrow scope will leave no room for the spiritually and socially disenfranchized; its structure will silently announce that "there is no room in the inn." The creative parish, on the other hand, will struggle to be flexible and strive to encompass its unconventional people for it knows that parish life, like life itself, is seldom neat and tidy and that there can be no distinction between the desirables and the undesirables. Moreover, the creative parish recognizes that in many ways it is in a unique position to provide a home away from home for many, a stabilizing haven for its "journeymen" or parishioners. The creative parish knows it has the power, some way or another, to make the alienated feel welcome, the estranged know of a new family and the fringe people become a part of the center.

At this point we can only suggest some alternatives to the old parish offerings, alternatives which provide a wide scope. (Part III will be more specific.) First, we should not, in our anxiety to help the broken, neglect to encourage the whole. Our intact families need a great deal of help and Andrew Greeley is right to insist that, besides good sermons and caring clergy, the thing most people dearly desire is to preserve their families and get all the help they can. As a church we have a further stake in good families: they tend to be good predictors of a healthy religious life. Again Greeley points out:

> Most of the serious research done on the phenomenon of religious identification (by Korte, Zelan, Capowitz, and Greeley) emphasizes the powerful influence of family background in the decision to disidentify religiously. The church, as Korte has pointed out, is an institution which emits many stimuli. Which stimulus one chooses to focus on in determining to identify or disidentify is a function of the psychological perspective one brings from the family experience to one's encounter with the church. Living apart from one's family and coming from a "broken" family or a family in which there is conflict or in which there is unusual strain between a person and his parents are powerful predictors of religious disidentification.[6]

Greeley goes so far as to say that "what counts religiously is not whether you have been 'secularized' but rather to whom you are married," and his answer to making people more religious is "make marriages happier."

It is also interesting to take a look at the results of a very large survey taken under the auspices of the United States bishops in their "Call to Action" program on the major needs and concerns of the family. What emerged were not primarily questions of abortion and birth control but these eight issues in order of concern:

1. *Support of Family Values.* Here husbands and wives wanted to be affirmed as being valuable. Here too they dearly wanted some kind of home devotions to bind them all together. They did not want the old family rosary for the kids would not tolerate it, but they wanted some religious action like the home Mass to give them something to remember. They all felt a real need for family prayer and the building up of family traditions around religion.
2. *Family Life Education.* Here they wanted skills. They felt alone in today's world of the secular expert. They wanted to learn skills in raising their children, in parenting well, in sex education.
3. *The Divorced.* Here was voiced the need (a) to be made to feel welcome in the church and (b) for assistance to the single parent.
4. *Communication Skills.* In today's alienating world they wanted to learn how better to communicate as husband and wife, as parents and teens, and even as family and church.
5. *Pressures Against Family Life.* How could they deal with those mass pressures that erode the family and over which they have no control? Things like television, ad-

vertising, high mobility, drugs, and alcohol? They did not like the fact that the family table has been replaced by the TV.

6. *Counseling.* They felt a need to have trusted professional counseling recommended by the parish.
7. *A Sense of Vocation.* Here they expressed a need to be regarded as having a true vocation as a family unit. They wanted opportunities to witness and to minister as a family.
8. *Single Parenting.* The ways and means of raising children when you're all alone.

The United States Catholic Conference has a long-range program to implement these wants and any parish would do well to tap these resources and to establish a new category of "Family Life Minister." There are, of course, the already tried and true family and couple programs today, from informal parish gatherings to the structures of Family Weekend, Evenings for Couples, and Evenings for Parents. There is Marriage Encounter, of course, marriage growth groups, family learning programs, and a host of people willing to come and help families grow. The creative parish will always have some family and marriage support programs.

Secondly, on the other end of the spectrum there are the growing number of divorced, separated, and remarried Catholics in any parish. They present a special challenge to the church at large as well as the local parish. It is sometimes easy to infer that such people are shallow and break their vows and commitments with ease. Some are like that, of course, but a far greater number have sweated out many years of trying to make a go of the marriage and have resorted to divorce only to keep their sanity and sometimes their very lives. And whether they are devout or lukewarm Catholics, guilt is a strong feeling to contend with. If you add to this a period of painful readjustment, caring for or visiting the children of a broken home, struggling financially, and now deprived of warmth, sexual fulfillment, and a living partner who cares you can sense the pain that the divorced, separated, and remarried must feel. Liberalizing divorce laws and social attitudes have not been a great boon to most of its beneficiaries in the place where it really counts: in affairs of the heart and home. This letter from one divorced man is typical:

> "My son, ten years and one day old, waves gamely as the Greyhound pulls out. He is bound 150 miles south to spend the long Fourth of July weekend with his mother. I stand in the hot parking lot, waving back until the bus fades far down into the stream of traffic. My son has made this strange shuttle many times before. He is one of the new legion of suddenly old children, paying in part for their parents' failures.
>
> I have stood here before and should not be too upset. Only this trip is different: His mother has remarried in the past month, and my son is going to live for the first time in a new house with a new, part-time surrogate father. The man is a complete stranger to me.
>
> Some people advise that I should be content. After all, if his mother is happier, the wisdom goes, won't that make a better situation for my son also? Perhaps. But it still galls and burns in the gut.
>
> My situation is better than most. Unlike nearly all divorced fathers, I enjoy joint custody: All major decisions regarding my son must be made by mutual agreement, and each parent is legally entitled to physical custody for half of each year. Because of school, the year is not split evenly: My son spends about 160 days each year with me, 200 with his mother. The summer, however, is nearly all mine, and the summer is the best of times. We have a good beach on Lake Champlain, a healthy garden, and my son plays centerfield for a baseball

team of eight-to-ten-year-olds that I coach. We won our opening game, and my son collected a double and a single. We celebrated at the local Pizza Hut. I should be satisfied, but I am not.

The 200 days away are 200 too many. More than half his year, more than half mine. And now there is this new man. Who is he? What is he like? Does that make any difference? By what right does he shelter my son under his roof more nights of the year than I do?

The government statisticians measure everything relentlessly. They tell us that one of two children born today will spend at least part of his life in a single-parent home. Most of these children will be reared by their mothers, since the courts still almost automatically, and unthinkingly, grant child custody in divorce to women. The fathers often become phantoms. They are limited to weekend visits, cut off from any role in vital choices of schooling, community and religion, vulnerable to termination of their visitation rights. American fathers, usually without much fuss, thought, or evaluation, routinely surrender the most basic rights of paternity in divorce proceedings. I wonder if this is so in other countries? Are the men of Greece, India, Japan, Brazil also so quick to yield their children? Why is the father's role and responsibility so diminished in America?

My immediate problem is that both his mother and I love our son. He is all we have to show for our marriage, except perhaps some aging photo albums from happier days, and our Solomon-like decision to split custody is really the best of a bad situation.

According to the practitioners of currently fashionable psycho-babble, we live in the best of times because more and more people are "being up-front" about their feelings and "doing their own thing." A system in which nearly everyone eventually winds up married to someone else is welcomed as a positive development, a sign of a new maturity in our society. Perhaps.

I should be grateful that my son and I are together as much

> as we are. We are not strangers to each other, nor, I hope, will we ever be. We are involved in each other's lives, and we have many fine times together. I shouldn't mind that he now lives with another man. After all this will give him a new "relationship" to develop. Learning to develop relationships is a vital survival skill in the new world a-building in America. I shouldn't mind.
>
> But the thing still seems wrong.[7]

Add to this, the dilemma of the Catholic who now more than ever needs community and, above all, the eucharist but finds himself or herself legally deprived of these things because of a remarriage. The last thing such people need, therefore, is an uncaring parish; the first thing they need is a sense of a place where wounds eventually can be healed. There are so many groups nowadays precisely for such people inspired by such people on the national scene as Father James Young and Sister Paula Ripple.[8] Any parish can have seminars to assist such people, a combination of legal, social, ecclesiastical and spiritual help.

Thirdly, our census survey showed us that more and more people are staying single—for the time being or permanently. Outside of the shallow jet-set crowd, the average Catholic (or any decent human being) soon tires of the singles bars and the one night stands. He or she knows deep down that life has more to offer. But except for commercial discos and hangouts, which amass their incredible collective wealth by feeding on people's anxieties, where can the singles go? Not just as a place, but as a resource for spiritual direction and guidance. If, in fact, they still resonate with their Catholic tradition, can they turn to a parish that gives off messages that all is for families and married couples only? The singles are in many ways in a cultural and spiritual limbo. A creative parish can at least acknowledge them and, at best, make them welcome and offer them a place of growth and commitment. After all, they are often people of talent and leadership and their ability to use their time well permits them to offer much to the parish that lets them know they are needed.[9]

Fourthly, there is the growing segment of alienated Catholics: those who have dropped out for one reason or another. Still, like money or in-laws, most people touched by Catholicism, can seldom do with it or without it. Somehow, no matter how long disenchanted with the Catholic church many former parishioners keep looking over their shoulders. Sometimes, all they need is a forum, a non-threatening opportunity to confront, talk, or simply ask. Once or twice a year the parish should offer that forum. It should advertise in the local papers and invite any Catholic who feels himself or herself alienated for whatever reason to come. Where it has been tried, it has been most helpful. Usually, those alienated Catholics who come tend to fall into three major categories, with many subcategories evident as well: those who are divorced or remarried and who therefore feel locked out of their church; those traditional Catholics who feel deeply betrayed by all of the changes which have altered and disfigured the church they knew and loved; those who have run into some insensitive priest or sister especially at such critically sensitive times as baptism or funerals. Whatever the reasons, there are a number of "former" or dropped-out Catholics who would welcome a forum to air their views. Occasionally the parish should open its doors to such alienated people, receive them without hidden agendas, just be honest with them, and, where called for, genuinely apologetic. This is evangelization in its best form. Many will come back, many won't, but all should at least be impressed with the humility of the endeavor and the message that someone cares.[10]

Finally, we consider here the senior citizens who have their needs: the physical and social needs to be fulfilled and the greater need to be needed. It is puzzling why the church ignores this latter need. The senior citizens are one of the great untapped resources in the church. These are people with experience, savvy, professionalism, and tried spirituality—and time. Seventy-five year old Lydia Bragger who is the national media coordinator of the Gray Panthers adds, "The church needs to involve older people. It must realize that older people have potential....Older people should be involved in every aspect of the church, but you can't tell them to be involved; you have to want them to become involved." Certainly the senior members of the church could fill much of the staffs at the average chancery, especially professional secretaries and lawyers. They could be trained to minister to the sick particularly in those senior citizens villages which dot this country. Perhaps, also, if ordination is ever to be extended in the Western world to the married, it might start here with the elderly in such villages. They would automatically become live-in priests caring for the many needs of their own. The concept probably would meet with least resistance here. Likewise, with their years of experience in the various secular fields, they, along with younger members, might be a part of any bishop's or parish's consulting boards.

I have always felt that parishes patronize and trivialize our senior citizens. They run all kinds of affairs for them and certainly no one would ever want to remove such things. But at times there is an uneasy feeling that *all* that we are doing is entertaining them and keeping them busy so they won't get lonely. We tend to treat them like elderly children who must be pacified, cared for, and patted on the head. Somehow we seem to be afraid to take them along (or follow them along) the one path in which they might excel and might most ardently desire: the path of holiness. We are so busy keeping *them* busy that we are not cultivating their most precious talent, the ability to be contemplatives. In the Eastern traditions an elderly husband and wife leave their homes and become official pilgrims sharing wisdom and seeking wisdom before they die. They are considered set apart and deferred to because of their age and their sacred pilgrimage. We of course, are in a highly youth-oriented society where old age is not only not reverenced but considered a high liability, almost an embarrassment. But it is the nature of the church to be prophetic and to turn on a different axis. Parishes should not be tricked into uncritically imitating all of the secular distractions for the senior citizens as their only approach. There should be a ministry to and by the elderly that respects a unique capacity to fathom the mysteries of the kingdom of God. We should devise programs that respect their spiritual journeys and give them opportunity to share with us the spiritual riches of their lives. We should cultivate in them and in the parish a sense of their being an "active cloister" which draws many graces and is an integral part of parish wholeness and holiness.[11]

There are all kinds of other groups to consider, but the principle remains the same: the creative parish with its many lay ministers must have a wide scope, a vision to see all, and arms to embrace all; it must make room for all. Meanwhile it will be relevant to share one final thought: a question of attitude. This says that a parish can have all kinds of programs for all kinds of people but, if, in the last analysis, such people do not share in the intimate liturgical and structural life of the parish, then all has been token.

Affirmation and acceptance will above all be found here. This is the test of sincerity. A parish that subtly denies a divorced person from being a lector, the separated from being a eucharistic minister, the single from being on the parish council, any minority person from being fully and equally a part of its full worship and organizational life — then it is making motions only and has yet to come to terms with its gospel spirituality. It must go back to learn from a Jesus who made his ministry especially directed to the outcasts and fringe people of his times and, when challenged, led him to exclaim, "The healthy do not need a doctor; sick people do. I have not come to invite the self-righteous to a change of heart, but the sinner" (Lk 5:31).

4

It should be evident from the foregoing that there is a persistent principle being applied, one that is a radical change from what we have operated by in the past centuries. We recall that the old principle declared that people must bend to the church and fit into a preconceived model. What we have been describing is a reversal of that. We have been applying our sacramental symbol which says that under the category of "scope" we are not out to get non-Catholics or the disenfranchised into the church to add another statistic to our national directory. Rather we stand there as the sign of the servant Christ. As Michael Warren so aptly expresses it, "The old task of ministry was to serve the assembled; the new task of ministry is to assemble those to be served." In short, we stand in reverence before the mystery of human freedom and forego the temptation to play the numbers game. We know there are many different paths, many different stories. We recall

Rahner's warning that there is no one single key that opens every door for every person and "there is no one single point for him from which everything can be surveyed, everything worked out, everything directed. . . . The humility and patience which goes with plurality. . . . belongs to the creaturely humility to be found in truly Christian pastoral work."[12] In short, we are taking the incarnation seriously:

> One of the great continuing dilemmas of the churches is that of effectively entering the lives of actual persons. In the person of Jesus we see most clearly that the law of salvation is incarnation: it is God's way of leading persons to himself. The task which must continue to guide the churches is that of allowing God to become more deeply present in the midst of human life through our own presence to life. But that seems to be the very point where we balk. We do not balk at the possibility of meeting God: we balk at the possibility of meeting our fellow men and women, and at the possibility that we will discover right there the astonishing presence of God.[13]

All this means that people need our ministry of help, guidance, and healing before any explicitly religious input or meaning. To put it all in a word, scope means that our first and primary ministry in the parish is the ministry of hospitality. As John Shea would put it, we must first gather the people of all walks of life and make them welcome, then tell and exchange our stories, and then break bread—in that order.

Notes for Chapter 8

1. Henri Nouwen, *Sojourners* (June 12, 1978), p. 9.
2. George Maloney, *National Catholic Reporter* (November 3, 1978), p. 16.

3. Henri Nouwen, *Clowning in Rome* (Image Books, 1979), p. 19.

4. Spoken by Charles Davis shortly before he left the church.

5. The suggestions mentioned in this section are all a part of our own parish rhythm.

6. Andrew M. Greeley, *Crisis in the Church* (Thomas More Press, 1979), p. 118. See also the excellent book *Family Life and the Church,* by David M. Thomas (Paulist Press, 1979).

7. William Colgan, "A Son Divided," *New York Times,* Op. Ed. page.

8. See *Ministering to the Divorced Catholic,* ed. James J. Young (Paulist Press, 1979).

9. See United States Catholic Conference's publication *The Single Experience.*

10. There is a very effective laboratory-workshop program for encountering the inactive church member offered by Lead Consultants Inc. of Pittstown, New York. The staff has worked with much success with many churches. Ours here in New Jersey was the first Catholic parish they worked with.

11. See Hugh Downes, *Thirty Dirty Lies About Old* (Argus Communications, 1979).

12. Karl Rahner, *The Christian Commitment* (Sheed and Ward, 1963), p. 93.

13. Michael Warren, "Evangelization of Young Adults," *New Catholic World* 222, no. 1331 (September/October 1979), p. 217. This whole issue, though devoted to the theme of young adults, is remarkable for the many fine articles on church and ministry that could be applied across the board.

9. Social Justice on the Quiet

1

Suppose you met someone shivering on a cold day because he had few clothes on and was hungry besides. You passed him by but not before saying, "Hey, there, get some warm clothes on and get a dinner somewhere"—-but provided neither. What would you think of that situation? Or suppose you went to a meeting and while there two women came in, the one gorgeously dressed and obviously well bred and the other poorly dressed and looking just this side of the cleaning woman. You said to the well dressed lady, "Come here and have a seat," and to the shabby woman, "You go and stand in the corner somewhere." What would you think of that?

We would probably react with mild outrage at the anomaly of the situation and remark how un-Christian such responses were. The more perceptive among us might recognize the two cases as literally taken from the examples found in chapter 2 of St. James' epistle. All of us would sense that there is more to the Christian life than words: deeds are needed as well. And when deeds are done for and with our needy brother and sister from faith, from the demands of the gospel, we have Christian social justice. Nothing could be more simple. On the contrary.

When we come to speak of our fourth foundation of the creative parish, social justice, nothing could be more complicated. And the complication is a peculiarly pastoral one.

It is not that the scripture is not clear. In Matthew 25 we will awesomely be judged according to how we fed, clothed, and visited the least of the brethren. St. John asks us, "How can God's love survive in a man who has enough of this world's goods yet closes his heart to his brother when he sees him in need?" (1 Jn 3:17); and he goes on to lecture us by saying, "little children, let us love in deed and truth and not merely talk about it. . . . one who has no love for the brother he has seen cannot love the God he has not seen" (1 Jn 3:18; 4:20). There are hundreds of examples in scripture that speak to us of social justice.

It is not that church teaching is not clear. In modern times, from the pioneering encyclical of Leo XIII in 1890 to that of Pope John Paul II in 1979, *The Redeemer of the Human Race,* the church has consistently reminded its members that faith requires those actions which redress wrongs and assist the unfortunate and oppressed. In Vatican II's *Pastoral Constitution on the Church in the Modern World* we read of "the birth of a new humanism, one in which man is defined primarily in terms of his responsibility for his brothers and for history" (n. 55); that Christians are called upon to "give witness of a living and mature faith . . . including its worldly dimensions, and by activating him toward justice and love, especially regarding the needy" (n. 21); that "the expectation of a new earth must not weaken, but rather stimulate our concern for cultivating this one" (n. 39). Most postconciliar documents have developed these same themes, such as the now famous Latin American Medellin documents of 1968 and the International Synod of Bishops of 1971 which reminded us that "unless the Christian message of love and justice shows its effectiveness through action in the cause of justice in the world, it will only with difficulty gain credibility with the men of our times. Action on behalf of justice and participation in the transformation of the world fully appear to us as a constitutive dimension of the preaching of the gospel, or, in other words, of the church's mission for the redemption of the human race and its liberation from every oppressive situation."

There is no ambiguity as to where the church stands on social justice.

It is not that the needs are not clear. We speak today of the Third World countries where the per capita national output is less than two thousand dollars a year, or what is termed a relatively low "physical quality of life" (Overseas Development Council's phrase). We now even speak of Fourth World countries, the poorest of the poor, whose per capita national output is less than three hundred dollars annually. Those figures mean nothing to us, but the cries of this man who has climbed up to the colossal statue of Christ of Corcovado do: "I have climbed up to you, Christ, from the filthy, confined quarters down there, with their stench of urine and typhoid fever, to put before you most respectfully these considerations: there are nine hundred thousand of us down there in the slums of that splendid city and the number keeps increasing. . . . And you, Christ, do you permit things like that? Why? Did you not come to help the world? . . . Christ do not remain here at Corcovado surrounded by divine glory. Go down there into the *favelas.* Come with me into the *favelas* and live with us down there. Don't stay away from us; live among us and give us new faith in you and in the Father. Amen."[1] Or we may be moved by the description of a man who has not studied poverty but who has lived it. Being poor, he says:

-Is witnessing the agony on your mother's face as she places hot cloths on your belly to quiet the hunger pains.

-It's watching your illiterate father succumb to alcohol because he is not equipped mentally or physically to raise seven children.

-It is stealing potatoes from the school cafeteria so that the family can eat supper that night.

-It is being put to bed early on Christmas Eve because there are no toys and no food.

-It is having your childhood's only birthday cake made without sugar or shortening.

-It is being called to the school cafeteria where your younger brother has falsely sworn that he brought vegetables from home in exchange for a hot lunch, and both you and he being brought to tears by a lecture on why children should never lie, and being sent back to your classroom without food.

-It's selling a dozen eggs needed by the family because you cannot bear the shame of not bringing your share of soft drinks for the school picnic.

-It is eating flour and meal mixed and cooked with hot pepper so that you won't eat too much.

-It's having your brother and sister drop out of the third grade because she doesn't have a dress and he is being laughed at for wearing a shortened version of your mother's tattered old coat.[2]

And this testimony comes from a man in our own United States.

It is not that cosmic issues are not clear. Military activity and the arms race devastate not only our material planet but the people on it as well. Every year, for example, massive diversion of resources into military ends and activities absorb about two-thirds of the gross national product of the poorer half of the world's population. Every year the world spends about 350 billion dollars for military purposes thus diverting needed money from social problems. Exports of major weapons to developing countries rose from 3 billion in 1970 to 7.3 billion in 1976. In short, one out of every six tax dollars is spent by the military to wage or prepare for war, yet most of the world is wanting the necessities of life. Here are words, all the more remarkable considering their source, from former U.S. Secretary of Defense, Robert S. McNamara: "Malnutrition saps their energy, stunts their bodies, and shortens their lives. Illiteracy darkens their minds and forecloses their futures. Preventable diseases maim and kill their children. Squalor and ugliness pollute and poison their surroundings. We are not talking about merely a tiny minority of unfortunates, a regretable but insignificant exception to the rule, but forty percent of the total population of one hundred countries."

Money diverted from their mouths into arms is an abuse that cries to heaven. That is why a Vatican statement to the United Nations on May 7, 1976 "condemned unreservedly" the arms race as an "act of aggression, which amounts to a crime, for . . . by their cost alone, armaments kill the poor by causing them to starve."

There is, then, no lack of clarity: scripture, the church, the needs, the issues are all there, open, apparent, observable to all. There is no doubt as to either the existence of social injustices that must be righted or the mandate we have to do so. There is no doubt about the guidance and the principles scripture and the church give us. There is no doubt, above all, about the urgency. Yet, there is the peculiar pastoral problem we have: why are we so uninformed and why are we so unmoved? Why do questions of social justice never appear on our adult education agendas and never spoken of from the pulpit? Why are we indifferent to social justice?

2

In seeking answers to these questions we come face to face with an unnerving irony: as far as social issues go, there are in fact several moral stances that members of the church are widely expected to know and to take—and for the most part do. Mostly such issues touch on family morality: abortion, divorce, euthanasia, and religious education. All Catholics are expected to agree on these matters, more or less, and they are issues persistently advertised, taught, discussed, and preached. Yet, oddly, Catholics are expected to have divergent views on the morality of war, racism, the arms trade, and aid to poor countries. And these issues are *not* advertised, taught, discussed, or preached. They are not alive for the average parish; they are nonissues, these incredibly profound questions which more than anything else on earth will determine our lives and alter our lifestyles. There is a virtual conspiracy of silence. As the King of Siam says, "It is a puzzlement!" Such a puzzlement is expressed in a summary statement of the general debate on the 1971 Synod of Bishops, and it is a real cry of frustration:

> How is it, after eighty years of modern social teaching and two thousand years of the gospel of love, that the church has to admit her inability to make more impact on the conscience of her people? . . . The faithful, and particularly the wealthy and more comfortable among them, simply do not see structural injustice as a sin, simply feel no obligation to do anything about it. . . . Sunday observance and the church's rules on sex

and marriage tend to enter the Catholic consciousness profoundly as sin. But to live like Dives with Lazarus at the gate is not even conceived as sinful.

Where do we find answers to the discrepancy of the clear call of the church and the clear deafness of her people? How do we alert indifferent parishes to a critical dimension of their lives? We might begin as we should: by not presuming pastorally that such unconcern is due to a real lack of good will. The people are not to be castigated nor confronted with issues they are not able to handle. Perhaps the first step for a parish is to try to see the hidden reasons buried in its heritage that might account for the indifference and moral lopsidednesses we all have. Some speculations—they are only that—are offered here.

1. *Social justice became categorized as somehow less "spiritual" and therefore less worthy of our attention.* Behind this statement lies a distinct Catholic interpretation of faith. For many centuries faith was seen primarily in intellectual terms, in terms of understanding (Anselm's "faith seeking understanding") and enlightenment. With this accent on faith as an illumination of the mind and the enlightened mind's assent to truth, then two results followed: first, the mind was seen as the "higher" part of man and the body "lower." It was a dualism that naturally tended to center on the soul alone and intellectual truth. It was a dualism that made faith a vertical projection of the mind and a kind of practicing for the Beatific Vision. It certainly had the tendency to take the focus off this evil world and its problems. Secondly, such a view of a faith that emphasized the mind's assent to truth did not necessarily carry with it any imperative to move into action, to *do* something.

The Protestant version of faith was no social improvement either. It tended to see faith as a trust between the person and God. People in this tradition tended to develop so intense a personal and devotional life that nothing could disturb them. No adverse circumstance was going to shake their trust in the Lord. As a matter of fact, the more injustice there was in the world, the more the faithful person turned inward to find comfort and security in Jesus. The net result of this view of faith was that if everything was so fully in the hands of God then the human equation in relieving the world's needs and answering the call of social justice is minimal if not absent altogether.

No wonder that at this juncture in our history both Catholic and Protestant theologians have come to the conclusion "that there seems to be something wrong with any theory that plays off God against all human and created agencies, so that trust in him involves a lack of trust in them."[3] Nevertheless the harm has been done and has left us with an indifference to social justice. A faith that relies solely on total trust in God is short on interest and one that defines itself as an assent to truth is short on action— and both have given rise to Marx's indictment that "religion is the opium of the people," lulling them to heavenly visions while the earth burns.

In this connection it is worth noting that, because they tend to hold these old views of faith to an extreme degree, evangelicals, Pentecostals, and charismatics are noticeably lacking in social sensitivity and social programs. They are far into the "Jesus and Me" syndrome. Recently there are signs that this lack has disturbed some of the leaders of these movements, and they are now trying to turn the picture around, but the road to awareness will be hard. Some time ago, for example, a newspaper article cited the anxiety of the professors of a well-known theological university whose students were unwilling to read since Jesus was enough for them. More recently, another article from a teacher told of her disenchantment with her bright twenty-year-old student who was "born again," and "since that day nine months ago, she has been off heroin and high on Jesus. She tells me that once you've found the Lord, you need look no further. Maybe that's why she got a D on the midterm . . . she stopped looking . . . It's all so simple, really. Acquire the Lord and live in a state of grace. What need is there to trouble with inquiry and scholarship? . . . Life becomes easier when you know at least God loves you, that he cares whether you pass the course, and that all you need do is call on him and he will, in his infinite wisdom, provide the answers on the final exam." The teacher is not being sarcastic, but perplexed and concerned that that kind of "faith" has absolved her student from contact with the real world. This is the kind of incident that gives us a clue as to why we have not traditionally reacted to social questions. The definition of faith we were trained in gave us reasons not to. The "head and heart" trip took us off course from the world.

As an aside here, we can appreciate the whole new axis of faith that the so-called liberation theology has tried to devise; for these South American theologians know what it is to live many centuries in suppressed acquiescence in the name of the Lord. They see that a faith that does not relate to action is bankrupt and plays into the hands of the oppressors. Redemption, in their eyes, cannot be separated from social, economic, and political factors. They are talking about St. Paul's "faith working through love" (Gal 5:6), a faith that does not intend to protect us from the world but to remake the world. There are real criticisms of liberation theology, but Avery Dulles, who himself offers some trenchant ones, is right when he says that the liberation theologians reworking of faith is to be praised for its demand that all Christains take seriously the obligation to work for a better political and social order.

But we don't want to get too far afield. We return to our first point: former definitions of faith tended to produce a tradition of "angelism"; that is, that somehow we were at our best when we were like angels: pure minds which gave assent to truth. Therefore only things of the mind were considered spiritual enough for consideration. Things of the body: food, housing, freedom, clothing, and employment were far too mundane to take seriously for a people whose faith was an interior assent, not an exterior messing around with a world that was not going to last anyway. With this understanding of faith, then, it stood to reason that "the church should not get involved in politics."

2. *Our Catholic American experience has left us socially timid.* Anyone who knows our history knows that Catholics entered the country as aliens to the Protestant ruling majority; that they initially were not allowed to hold public office, buy property, or even settle in most of the colonies. There is a long history of Know-Nothingism, the Ku Klux Klan, and the American Protective Association that tells of long-standing antipathy towards Catholics right up to the contemporary climate that makes "anti-Catholicism the anti-Semitism of the liberals." The Protestant Crusade has left its mark which even the election of the first Catholic president has not erased. Such a history has united strange humanistic bedfellows who have formed coalitions against what they conceive to be Catholic power. Ethical and social issues are always open for discussion and legislative political maneuvering—unless the Catholic church is involved as a moral presence or advocate. The issues automatically become "religious" ones thereby provoking the unanswerable challenge of violation of the separation of church and

state. All of this has had the net effect of a loss of confidence for Catholics on the one hand, and, on the other, of trying to prove how American they are by not being united on any issue. The collective conscience and awareness have been intimidated and, as a consequence, large social issues do not find soil for discussion in Catholic parishes.

3. *Secularism's triumph has segregated religion into another sphere.* As our society grows more and more secular, as high specializations abound and the legitimacy of secular efforts and beliefs are rightly acknowledged and honored, then religion is inadvertently pushed into the periphery of political and economic spheres. A world increasingly autonomous from religious influence feels it does not need any church to look over its shoulder or interfere. The result is, as one writer puts it, that "the legitimate autonomy of the political arena, expressed in the principles of religious liberty and separation of church and state, raises serious questions about the possibility of common Christian action for justice."[4] This kind of political atmosphere is also likely to inhibit any sure and certain plunge into questions of social justice.

4. *Contemporary complexity makes any parish hesitate.* Social issues are not simple today, if they ever were. They involve global circumstances and technology so complex, refined, tangled, and rarified that even the so-called experts are baffled or confused. Data is so incredibly complex that it confounds even our computers. Life is not so intimately joined on all levels that no one can see and assess it all. Large corporations, world banks, governments, industry are so vast and their power so great that the average person cannot understand or cope. Perspective is hard to get and a certain and sure answer, unanimously grasped and taught, is hard come by. We have moved too far and too fast for simple answers:

> In his struggle to know, to control, and to direct his natural environment — earth, water, and air; cold, heat, and energy; plants and animals; distance and time — Western man created, step by accelerating step, a new social environment: from hunting bands, nomadic tribes, farming villages, city-states, nations, and feudal empires he moved to multinational economic and political bodies and blocs; from barter and simple markets to commercial partnerships, stock companies, legal contracts, trade agreements, cooperatives and industrial corporations, banks, insurance and pension funds, stock exchanges; from yeomanry and artisan guilds to labor unions. . . . Today's householder no longer wrestles in heroic solitary struggle via windmill, well, and campfire, with water, draughts and darkness, cold and heat. He deals rather with the local utility company, which deals with labor unions, environment, and planning boards, federal rate and energy commissions; and they in turn with multinational corporations, OPEC, and eventually with the Arab League and the United Nations. To get meat and milk, potatoes and transport, the family no longer trails deer and digs the soil, corrals cattle and lassos horses. They drive to the supermarket and call up the airline, which in turn bargain with General Foods and General Motors, the Farm Bureau, and Farm Workers, the Federal Aviation Authority, congressional committees, White House staff, and Madison Avenue.[5]

If such is the ordinary, commonplace complexity of our daily lives, who has the boldness to make positive statements about political and social justice and where in fact such justice really lies? Not that we are without principles or genuine help or clear church teaching; it's just that global complexity gives us pause even with these.

5. *Fear of being considered radical or alienating.* Insistent social sermons will provoke and alienate many. There are all kinds of liberals and conservatives in any congregation

who will take different interpretations from what is said. Experiences have often proven bitter in the Vietnam war when peace signatures were sought in church vestibules causing nasty confrontations between Catholic hawks and doves. People tend to feel that they come to church on Sundays to be comforted not confronted, and certainly not to be exposed to some "liberal" priest's politics with no chance for public rebuttal. Few clergy therefore are willing to split their congregations right down the middle with statements that unfairly may align them with Ronald Reagan or Jane Fonda. It is this fear of being considered radical or the pastoral fear of becoming ineffective by alienating his people that keeps social issues, except in general terms, absent from the pulpit. Courage is surely needed, but the courage that leads not destroys, and sometimes it's hard to tell the difference.

6. *The church itself may be a part of the problem.* We come from an old European heritage of church power, wealth, status, and leadership. We have been aligned both in Europe and in America and elsewhere with current political structures and have often benefited from them. This has led us into the habit of not questioning the social system that has been to our benefit or looking into social matters which might backlash and force us to make fundamental changes. Our credibility has not always been firm and to take a strong stand will mean more than words; it must mean a radical alteration of our own lifestyles and church structures. A cardinal of Bolivia was right when he said, "the church could possess her wealth and her territory in the past with a quiet conscience, but today, in face of hunger and deprivation of so many people, this can no longer be done without sin."[6] We remain a part of the problem and prophetically inhibited until church policies and structures and the lifestyles of clergy and reli-

gious take the lead in living social justice, not in writing about it. It is one of the contemporary glories of the South American church, so long on the side of oppressive dictatorships and a debilitating status quo, that it has thrown itself in word and action squarely on the side of the poor and oppressed. It has begun its prophetic action for social justice and so can freely give sermons on it. Until we act in like manner, our silence betrays, not a lack of clear principles to declare, but a lack of heart to live, social justice.

7. *Finally, we have been raised with a domesticated liturgy.* Here we share the thoughts of an interesting meeting held at Notre Dame in June of 1979. It seemed an innocent enough meeting for it was the Eighth Annual Conference for Pastoral Liturgy. One would think that the discussions would center around singing or rubrics or how to celebrate, but not this time. The theme was on "Service: Community Prayer and Community Justice." The interesting thing was that the scholars there received the same treatment as any parish priest would have expected had he preached on the same subject: fewer people came, the mood was tepid and some even walked out at a talk by Father Dan Berrigan. Nevertheless the participants boldly went on demonstrating through theology and scripture, the intimate connection between community justice and worship. They said that our liturgy and our theology are too tame, too ivy towered and must be brought down into real life in a world that is hungry, oppressed, and enslaved.

Still, that old pastorally sensitive point kept coming up in the get-togethers afterwards and in the public question sessions: how do we respond to the needs of social justice and at the same time not alienate our congregations? How do we get beyond a liturgy that makes people feel good and affirms them, but leaves them without a challenge to feed the hungry and visit the sick? How can the liturgy overcome the social apathy of the parish? Everyone agreed that social justice should be integrated into the liturgy, but no one could answer how. Everyone admitted the tension, the problem. As one said:

> If I mount the pulpit with scripture alone in my hands, if I limit my preaching to the broad biblical imperatives, if I simply repeat scriptural slogans like "man does not live by bread alone"; "My peace I give to you"; "Seek first the kingdom of God"; "Love your neighbor as yourself"; "Wives, be subject to your husband"; then hungry stomachs will stay bloated, the arms race will escalate, dissidents will rot in political prisons, blacks will return to their slavery, and women will continue to be second-class citizens in much of the world. After all, it is not only the heathen who are responsible for oppression. The oppressors, large and small, often break the eucharistic bread with us.[7]

Yet, even after saying this, the speaker came back to the question of how can one preach all this without offending the people. How forceful and concrete dare we be?

These are some of the reasons why we do not deal at all or comfortably with social justice in our parishes. The reasons show us how we acquired an almost ingrained resistence to overt reminders of the world's distress or social confrontations. Besides, we all have to deal with our own pressured world of shrinking dollar, cut backs, less energy, unemployment, and recession. Yet all of this does not negate the fact that we are the minority haves in a world of majority have nots. It does not negate the fact that, with so essential a gospel imperative to care for our brothers and sisters, the question of social justice must be faced by any parish worth its sacramental sign of the compassionate Christ.

3

It would seem that we are faced with a dilemma: we admit that social justice is a foundation for the creative parish—it's too fundamentally gospel not to be—and we admit that to get it going is difficult. How do we proceed? Outside of becoming a disturbing (and disturbed) revolutionary, the priest and lay leaders can work out some broad structures that may begin to sensitize the people and give an unmistakable tone to the parish as one which cares. Four are suggested here.

Encourage emphatic but nonthreatening programs. For example, powerful visuals hung around church or hall now and then can provoke subliminal interest and compassion. On the last Sunday of the month have a food collection. Place some tables in the sanctuary and have the people place food packages there before Mass—including such needed goods as paper towels, diapers, napkins, and cleaning aids. Families might encourage their children to prepare the bags and actually do the placing in the sanctuary. Senior citizens days of recollection followed by a parish dinner and entertainment, hosted by the teenagers, can give another dimension to the lives of both. Clothing drives, communal anointings, adopting Vietnamese families or assisting the Boat People are all legitimate ways that any parish can use to reach out to the less fortunate. These things are not handling the root of the problems, but they are social services that can sensitize some people who might want to tackle that later. One further suggestion concerns the children. Most parishes have children's envelopes whether they have a school or not; and the total sum of these does not really amount to that much on a given Sunday. It would be a good teaching lesson in social justice if the parish would announce that from henceforth the money from the children's envelopes will never be used for the parish itself but rather will be diverted into some formal organized charity such as Bread for the World. (Bread for the World will send acknowledgement and thank you letters which might be then shared with the parish.) Then at the end of each month have the children themselves open, calculate, and deposit the money before it is sent away. It is not much, but it is meaningful and helps towards alerting young minds to their needy peers throughout the world. Again, it is not this or that program that says it all; it is simply the power of their cumulative effect to raise consciousness.

Form and publicly recognize new parish organizations that cater to social needs. Some parishes have a Vincent de Paul society or the Knights of Columbus; they may be flourishing or inactive. In any case, new styles for service are needed and new names. Two suggestions come to mind. One is what might be called the Samaritan Ministry. Here men and women, on behalf of the parish community, care for and assist those in need. This may be a question of bringing communion to the shut-ins or those in the hospital or nursing homes or riding them to clinics or doctor's appointments. What marks them off from general goodwill activities is their life of prayer, their communal sharing, their study and their willingness to engage in a ministry of healing prayer. Another might be called the Lazarus Ministry. Some parishes have made the decision to let their churches be open for wakes. The body is brought to the church the evening before and then the Mass of Christian burial is celebrated on the next morning at the regular community Mass. The Lazarus Ministry assists in the arrangements and provides for the physical needs and comfort of the family and visitors. There are as many suggestions as creative ideas. Again, the point is an official sensitizing for many people to the needs of others.

Restore the sacraments as prophetic signs. Sacraments are signs, symbols of greater realities and are at the heart of the church's life as a worshiping community. The sacraments, as communal actions, touch the head and the heart and have the power to inspire social activity if properly explained and celebrated. The symbol of each sacrament points beyond the sanctuary to the world. Baptism, after all, is not just for the members of the church but is a sign of that grace that God holds out for all. The eucharist shows the radical source of unity of all people for as the bread is made up of many grains brought together so is the community; and, likewise, as bread reaches its highest purpose and function when it is broken and distributed, so does the community. The sacrament of reconciliation by its very nature speaks of a wholeness for the hungry, the sick, and the needy. Confirmation tells of charismatic concern for and service to others; witnessing in word and in deed is its chief characteristic and its underlying social thrust. The sacrament of the sick proclaims healing to a fractured people within and without the community; it celebrates in a special way also all those who care for the sick and who minister to them.

Matrimony and holy orders, above all, are *the* social sacraments not merely because they deal with human relationships but because they deal with them in the faith terms of tolerance, forgiveness, caring, and growth. So there is a profound social relevance to all of the sacraments, and the wise parish loses no opportunity both to teach and to celebrate them in such a context.

The point made about the eucharist being a source of unity and sharing among all people was emphasized particularly by the last International Eucharistic Congress which had as its motto: "The Eucharist and the Hungers of the Human Family." And the book by theologian Monika Hellwig, *The Eucharist and the Hunger of the World,*[8] again underlines this theme. These broader themes can be found in a fuller theology of the parish; as such they can be pastorally explored as a means to sensitizing people to the awareness that the story of Dives and Lazarus is more than a parable: it is both invitation and judgment.

Promote an actual social ministry in the parish. Going the route of a social ministry enables the parish to deal with smaller groups who hopefully might influence the larger congregation. What is involved here is more than social service as described above. This has a more formal and more professional thrust. The members are expected to study and get proper formation and understand not only the large issues but the best tactics for achieving a just society. Social ministry in this context is "primarily concerned with the development (training, enabling, energizing, motivating, empowering) of the people doing the action."[9] And the key concept here, of course, is not that such social ministers are trained to do a social action *for* someone but *with* someone so that he or she learns how to meet and improve a situation. The focus here is not to overthrow by revolution an existing institution or compete with it by establishing a substitute system, but to change and reform it so that it is more just. The problem often is that the system itself is defective and even perhaps immoral, not the people involved who may not even be aware of the system's built-in justices. The system itself must be transformed in the light of the gospel.

A case in point here was the unusual pastoral letter written by the Catholic bishops of the chronically poor Appalachian region of our country. The bishops asked why the people of Appalachia were always oppressed. When the mines were working and they had jobs, they were exploited. When the mines were shut down they were unemployed. When the mines reopened their plight was the same. The bishops went out of their way to insist that the problem does not necessarily lie in the lack of generosity of the more successful people or the ill will of those who run the large corporation. Rather what is evident here is the root evil in the system itself. Built into it are principles that will always hurt the workers no matter what and that must be changed. For instance, the bishops pointed out two operating principles in the system that are insensitive to the workers. The first they mentioned is "technological rationalization" which means that all ways of efficiency and planning are explored to get maximum effort. Each factor is scientifically examined to get a better operation going—every factor except the people. Decisions concerning them are made as if they were things, inanimate pieces of the overall corporate machinery. Technological rationalization is constituted in the very soul of the system and it must change so that people too are an essential and alive consideration in decision making. This technological rationalization is the same thing as Lionel Rubinoff's "functional rationality": "Here all quality is translated into quantity. Here the human being is dissolved into needs and wants. Here people tend to become objects, appear as items in an inventory, and serve the needs and efficiency of the system. The solution of functional problems dominates over the fate of individuals."[10]

The second operating principle to the harm of the people, the bishops pointed out, is the "maximization of profit" as the *only* consideration in decision making. This is not greed operating or heartlessness. It is just that this maximization of profit is the sole factor that determines what happens in the corporation; it excludes any consideration of the human equation. It is these two principles, the bishops argue, not some monstrous corporate Simon Legree, that cause grief to the people of Appalachia. Until the system itself is reformed and transformed the people's plight will never be improved. Social ministries can be trained to deal with such things and act on them in concert with people of good will who are seeking social justice. It is hoped that their witness, blessed and supported by the parish, will bring to the attention of the congregation a dimension that might otherwise be too sensitive to broach consistently or too distant to be noticed.

It is recommended, of course, that preachers do get bolder and preach more often than they do now on such pressing issues without offense or accusation. There may be more avenues of a more direct approach in those parishes which have kind of taken a one note stand or a central theme stand. For example, some parishes gear their whole lifestyle to the new rite of adult Christian initiation with all of its ramifications. Some parishes are styled charismatic. Those parishes so tied into a central notion might be experiments to watch in the area of social justice.[11]

4

We conclude this part which has dealt with the four foundations of the creative parish: ministry, spirituality, scope, and social justice. These four foundations are hardly complete or exclusive. They do, however, provide some signs of what a creative parish might look like and what it might deal with. They give a direction for the parish that is aware that Christ is ever incarnated anew in every place where "those who know" form the church. They are principles, not programs, that should help the parish that is a sacrament to be as authentic as it can be. The next and final part turns to the personal experience of one parish to see how such principles might be translated, to an experiment in pastoral theology.

Notes for Chapter 9

1. Quoted in Walbert Buhlmann, *The Coming of the Third Church,* (Orbis Books, 1977), p. 125.
2. Words of J. Carl Cook in a radio broadcast, quoted in *National Catholic Reporter* (June 15, 1979), p. 14. For a penetrating film on the horrendous crises that face underdeveloped countries see *Five Minutes to Midnight* (World Focus Ltd., London).
3. Avery Dulles, "The Meaning of Faith Considered in Relationship to Justice" in *The Faith That Does Justice,* ed. John C. Haughey (Paulist Press, 1977), p. 28.
4. David Hollenbach, "A Prophetic Church and the Catholic Sacramental Imagination," in ibid., p. 237.
5. Joseph Gremillon, *The Gospel of Peace and Justice* (Orbis Books, 1976), pp. 25, 26. This whole book is a real compendium of social insights and contains the major encyclicals and postconciliar documents.
6. Quoted in Buhlmann, *Third Church,* p. 121.
7. Walter Burghardt, quoted in *A.D. Correspondence* (July 14, 1979). For another expression of the dilemma see "Of Many Things," *America* (July 21, 1979).
8. Monika Hellwig, *The Eucharist and the Hunger of the World* (Paulist Press, 1976).
9. Harry Fagan, *Empowerment* (Paulist Press, 1979), p. 10. An excellent how-to booklet, full of common and gospel sense for any starting social ministry program.
10. Lionel Rubinoff, quoted in Gregory Baum, *The Social Imperative* (Paulist Press, 1979), p. 55. See also David Hollenbach, *Claims in Conflict: Retrieving and Renewing the Catholic Human Rights Tradition* (Paulist Press, 1979).
11. For an article that tries to come to terms with world issues on the parish level, see Francis X. Meehan and William Mattia, "The Arms Race and the American Parish," *America* (September 22, 1979).

PART III

PASTORAL POSTSCRIPTS

10. Pastoral Postscripts

1

We have finished our exploration of the background elements of the creative parish. The book therefore should end here and perhaps prudence demands it. Still, the introduction identified me as a parish priest of twenty-five years. Is there, then, something to share that helps translate what we have written into practical terms? Or is it a question of "those who can't, teach"? It is an unsettling question but a fair one. The best response I can offer is a series of random material in the appendices that follow this chapter. They contain a lot of practical ideas drawn from the theoretical ideals. Studying them should give a flavor, a taste for the translation process. Nor should the many ideas already scattered throughout the book be neglected.

This chapter contains a compendium of approaches—they pretend to be nothing more than that—that I have used over the years, approaches that might be designated under the twin titles of "Policies That Build" and "Touches That Bind." The first phrase refers to the truism that there will always be some policies that by their nature build up as there are those which by their nature tear down. The second phrase means that each of us has his or her own personal style and touch that spills over into ministry and binds people into community. Remember that I write from a leadership point of view. I wish that I could dazzle you with genius and inventiveness here, but, as Cervantes wrote, "I wish this book, as the child of my brain, to be the most beautiful, the liveliest, and the cleverest imaginable. But I have been unable to transgress the order of nature, by which like gives birth to like." So, I merely offer a check list of approaches, the best I know, with a brief commentary on each item.[1]

1. *Education.* By definition this is a policy that builds and it is most critical. People have to know what is going on, they have to have reasons for changes, for believing, for coping with their lives. They are apt to be especially sensitive when cherished religious beliefs and traditions are tampered with. Education is not the whole answer and might not make converts out of many people, but it does put things in context. I have found this area of education to be the most neglected among the average parishioners. It is either not given at all or too superficially. I am still amazed, when I talk to groups, that even in this day they are asking questions that are no longer relevant, questions which should have been answered fifteen years ago. And once things are explained and put in perspective you can almost see the light go on, the relief that sets in. No parish can exist with vigor that does not provide some kind of ongoing education whether through adult classes and seminars, sermon series, open dialogues, or the generous use of Sunday bulletin stuffers.[2]

2. *Openness.* This policy says that we must respect those who can't or won't see our vision. We should not back them into a corner with an either-or confrontation. Either we have the offertory dance or novenas, the bible vigil or the rosary, banners or statues. The parish, like the universal

church, should practice pluralism within its ranks too. The church is quite large enough to contain both communal and private confessions, scapulars and "Jesus Is Lord" bumper stickers, guitar Masses and devotions to Our Lady of Fatima. People should not be made to feel out of it because they cannot accept the style or philosophy of the parish. They may feel uncomfortable but should not feel excluded.

3. *Professionalism.* By this is meant that things should be done as well as possible. Take, for example, the liturgy since that is the most public display which affects most people. People may not care for certain changes or agree with them but they will be tolerant if the liturgy is well done with care, devotion, and sincerity. It's a kind of law of nature that says that something well done may not win converts but will lessen prejudice. Besides, something well done is in fact its own best advertisement. The parish has to be willing to invest time and money towards this policy.

4. *People investment.* This does not mean merely to trust and work with the people. It also means that the creative parish must be willing to budget its money to educate people away from the parish. There are so many offerings in the field of religion and related studies. There are endless workshops, courses, and seminars. Parishes should sponsor people to attend such things. There need not be any immediate relevance or application, for in time there will always be some enrichment which will surface in the parish in some form or other.

5. *Zoning.* Every parish should be zoned into smaller segments. Even if the parish is already comparatively small it should still be divided into natural neighborhood sections for reasons both immediate and for the future. For one thing, zoning automatically groups neighborhoods. This makes it easier to choose area captains, parish council

representatives, recruit census takers, line up neighborhood visitations, cull families to serve the weekend liturgies, and a host of other practicalities. (If the parish uses an addressograph plate or the like, it is convenient to include the zone number somewhere so that it becomes an easy matter to run off index cards and pull out all the same numbers resulting in a handy file of neighborhood families.)

Zoning will prepare the parish for the possibility of another growing phenomenon: the neighborhood church. It is in these smaller "parishes within the parish" that renewal can take better hold and true leadership emerge. This is not entirely novel. There used to be the old Christian Family Movement cells and modern day cursillo and marriage encounter groups are designed along the same lines.

A new and interesting development are the hispanic *communidades eclesiales de base* or basic church communities (CEB). These subcommunities tend to incorporate a political vision of the gospel which challenges social injustice (the obvious influence of liberation theology). Such communities have mushroomed in South America and are now flourishing in certain key United States cities. They were openly recognized by the Medellin Conference of 1968 which spoke of them as "the initial cell of the church and the radiating center of its evangelizing effort." Pope Paul VI went so far as to call them "a hope for the universal church."

It is also worth quoting the words of the General Synod of Bishops meeting in Rome in 1971. They were speaking about the whole notion of zoning and parish subdivisions in general: "Let priests . . . strive with great prudence and pastoral charity to form communities which are imbued with apostolic zeal and which will make the church's missionary spirit present everywhere. Small communities, which are not opposed to parish or diocesan structures, ought to be inserted into the parochial or community in such a way that they may serve it as a leaven of missionary spirit. The need to find apt forms of effectively bringing the gospel message to all men, who live in differing circumstances, furnishes a place for the multiple exercise of ministries." Such smaller groupings are an effective and positive reaction to large and impersonal parishes and lack of clergy; and they do reflect the ideals of shared responsibility and ministry. The parish that is zoned is at least mechanically open to move in this direction.

6. *Communications.* A sense of community, coresponsibility, and ministry is best served by good mechanical as well as personal communications. A parish that is willing to invest its money in a basic communication system understands this: a mimeograph, plate maker, addressograph, electronic stenciler, folding machine, and census file. These all help in speeding information through the mail which is still the cheapest way of reaching all parishioners, the good, bad, and indifferent. No revolutionary would be caught without such basics. The gospel revolutionary should not be less committed.

Communications work both ways and so there has to be some legitimate means for the parish at large to dialogue with the pastor and staff. One way is to have all parish council meetings open to the public and held on times convenient for all (maybe after the biggest Mass on Sunday?). Another is to have a suggestion box or mail slot available. Another idea is to have a regularly scheduled dialogue Mass on Sundays.

Another in-depth means of talking and listening is to develop the census form. A census form should take more than statistical information. It should have pages that provide space for opinion, suggestions, and criticism. A few years ago we designed what we think is a very good census form. We don't know how sociologically professional it was, but it certainly met our purposes. For example, it offered such "complete the following statements" as: "Something I've always wanted to say to the pastor is. . . ." "I think the parish should. . . ." "I think the biggest problem we have to face today is. . . ." In categories that graduated from very good, good, fair, poor, and indifferent people had a chance to check them off in regards the following: "My feelings about St. Mary's is. . . ." "The sermons given by Father Bausch are. . . ." "The music, lectors, CCD program, banners, flowers, organizations are. . . ." Then we included opportunities to serve on committees, get involved with programs, and offer particular talents. For the full draft of the census form consult the appendix.

7. *The Parish Booklet.* Every year we put out a parish booklet containing all of our programs and policies and plans for the year (September to June) plus the parish calendar. The booklet carries all kinds of information and serves as a directory for needs. It is hard work and takes a lot of planning, but it is worth it. It lists the names of the many, many people involved. Each year we get new faces and new people in order to prevent cliques and to share the responsibilities. The parish booklet provides a new theme each year which rallies the parish and the booklet is sent to every registered parishioner. Some themes and titles have been, "The Year of Celebration," "The Year of Faith," "The Year of Community," "The Year of Vision."

8. *Liturgy: Variety and Courtesy.* Every parish has its weekend Mass schedule. We have adopted the policy of making this a flexible arrangement to meet the needs of the people. Therefore: on the first Sunday of every month at the 12 noon Mass we have a High Mass with the tra-

ditional choir. On the second Sunday of every month at the 5 P.M. Mass we have a teen liturgy suited to the young people. On the third Sunday of every month at the 12 noon Mass there is "dialogue Sunday" when the celebrant simply approaches the lectern at homily time and asks what they want to talk about and what are the questions they would like to ask, things they would like to challenge. Very helpful, often entertaining, always informative. Finally, on the last Sunday of every month we have the Folk Choir in the morning and our Moppet Mass at 5 P.M. followed by refreshments and balloons in the parish hall. We have a brochure made up which gives directions to those in charge. The children do the readings, pantomime the gospel, bring up the gifts, sing in the Moppet Choir, decorate the church, bring forth the vestments and sit around the celebrant in the sanctuary for the homily which is always a story. Courtesy in reference to the liturgy reveals itself in the fact that at the end of each month we list the various celebrants for the coming month's Masses. We also rotate the celebrants so that they have a different set of Masses each month.

9. *Communality.* This refers to our policy of always having the sacraments (and indeed any significant function) celebrated before, by, and with the community.[3] This means baptisms, reception of converts, marriage vow renewals, sometimes marriages, funerals, anointing of the sick, and anything else that the parish should be aware of and a participant in take place at the community Masses. The catechetical value needless to say is enormous.

10. *Money.* A sensitive area but one that speaks to many people about the church and about the parish, for better or worse. No enterprise can run without money, but there must be certain pastoral policies that build up not tear down here. Some suggestions which not all may agree with

are: there should never be a second collection, much less a third or fourth one. Four collections simply mean four quarters instead of one dollar. Even when the missionary comes for the annual appeal the one collection policy should still prevail. The creative parish should have enough communal faith to give that Sunday's entire collection to the missions. Mandated second or third collections from the chancery should be dealt with in other ways in order to leave the one collection intact.

Secondly and importantly, the sole offertory collection should be grounded in faith. In the one money talk I give shortly after arriving at a parish I ask that people give one hour's wages, consciously and religiously. People should consecrate any hour of their choice to the Lord and that is their gift to him. When the collection is placed before the altar it then has meaning.

Thirdly, do not take stipends for baptisms, funerals, confirmations, and weddings. People may still insist on giving something, but it is nice to have a policy that says that this is the people's parish and they are entitled to all celebrations in virtue of their status. Fourthly, there should never (almost never) be money-raising events before or after Mass as we explained in previous pages.

Finally, we have come to the time in our current rhythms of revival to consider some radical moves in regard to money. When a parish has to have six or seven bingos a week to keep alive then the cost is too high. Certainly too high to keep the parish open as it presently stands. The money tail is now wagging the ecclesiastical dog, and something is very wrong. Certainly the image is all wrong. Radical realignment may have to be considered, such as selling some property, assessing the more affluent parishes, or going back to truly simple living styles, a gospel way of life that is poor. We have sinned so much on the other side that even enforced evangelical poverty is not the worst image of the Catholic church to present to the world. When all is said and done, people tend to vote with their pocketbooks. If there is a spirit of love, openness, and service, the money problem will be less threatening, less preoccupying.

11. *Pride of Place.* There are certain symbolic actions and changes that speak of style and policy that build. Some parishes, for instance, have ceased calling themselves St. Paul's parish and have changed the title to St. Paul's community or St. Paul's family. It is not much, but it is trying to say something about the way the parish looks at itself. Our own parish motto attempts to say a lot: "A Christian Community in the Roman Catholic Tradition." As community we join the whole human race in its journey towards betterment and towards God. Within that universal community we represent a peculiarly gospel stance towards life and within that gospel stance we move within Roman Catholic expressions, aspirations, and interpretations. Long ago we changed the word rectory to parish house to suggest a wider sense of community. Pride of place also refers to the common effort at keeping the material building expressive of its spirit: tasteful banners, flowers, gracious ushers, prepared music, a public bulletin board in the church vestibule, a guest register book there for visitors (who later will receive a courtesy letter in the mail), photographs of our activities—all coalesce to announce that "people live here, love here, celebrate here. It's a nice place to be, to belong to. Welcome!"

12. *Openness to the larger community.* True to our sacramental definition, we should be open to the outside community and be a living sign that we promote whatever is human. This means letting the parish be open to any outside group for meetings; it means giving welcome to any

group, secular or religious, which is promoting any part of peace, justice, and truth.

Thus, an even dozen samplings of Policies that Build, mechanical devices and practical approaches that help translate principles into reality. We move on to the more personal Touches that Bind in the next section.

2

13. *Being Present.* Foremost among the touches that bind is the obvious one that the priest and/or staff must be present when the people are present. This usually means before and after every Mass; it means endless meetings; it means all the ways that we are father, mother, brother, and sister to all.

14. *Saturday Night Dinners.* Subtitled: for those who can arrange it. Like most parishes we have Saturday vigil Masses. Ours are at 5 and 7 which means that we cannot conveniently eat before or between. So we eat afterwards, around 8:30. This being so, we decided to institute the policy of inviting a couple from the parish to join us each Saturday. We devised a letter of invitation, and we send it out well in advance. The people are thrilled in spite of the fact that I do the cooking. Over drinks, food, and fellowship we learn so much about one another and a real family bond is formed. An excellent touch that binds!

15. *Gatherings.* This refers to the policy of openness and welcome and interaction among us all. For instance, on the last Sunday of every month we have a mini-breakfast, hosted by various neighborhood groups, after the main Mass. Free coffee, cocoa, donuts mixed with chitchat and

neighborliness is the formula. Another thing: we have no movies in town so on certain winter Sundays we show films to provide the kids a chance to have fun, dad a chance to watch the football game, and mother the cheapest baby sitting in town.

We have mentioned our policy of having wakes in church and the Lazarus committee which provides hospitality to family and visitors. Parish picnics (our annual 10¢ Labor Day Picnic is famous in the area: where can you buy hot dogs, corn, balloons, kites, and beer for ten cents?), parish trips, easter egg hunts on the lawn after all the Masses on Easter—all are ways to interact, all are variations of the same theme: we are God's celebrating people.

16. *The Children.* The children are not, of course, a policy; but we have spoken elsewhere of the married, divorced, the separated, the singles. What about the children? Are there policies here that are worth sharing? With the children our overriding philosophy is that religion is caught not taught. Therefore we try to provide emotionally as well as spiritually edifying activities. We try to make pleasant associations for them so that even the products of the most religiously indifferent parents will have a good feeling about the church. We do have once a week CCD classes which we consider totally counterproductive—if it were not for all the other contexual things of the parish. In itself one hour CCD class is an isolated and negative fact of parish life as far as the children are concerned. But place it in the larger context of a living parish, make it but one piece of the larger, overall mosaic of community, then it has something to say.

What context do we offer? There are the overnight retreats whereby, on different nights, the boys and girls of the fifth and sixth grades bring their sleeping bags and spend overnight at the parish house (we take seventh and eighth graders away). There is a religious program, but we suffer no illusions. They are dancing with anticipation of the inevitable pillow fight and morning breakfast at McDonald's. We anticipate that the good feeling, staying overnight at "Father's House," having fun in a churchy setting will prevail in the long run. We have mentioned already the Moppet Masses, the blessing of their pets. On All Saints Day we have them all come to weekend liturgy dressed in costume; their obligation is to look up their saint's life and tell the story to the assembly. At Advent time they paint Christmas scenes on our clear parish hall windows. The boys of the seventh grade and the girls of the sixth grade have a fine sex and character education course offered to them.

17. *Flexibility*. This is the final touch that binds. Paradoxically, it says that we should not in fact bind either people or systems. It says that every once in a while the parish should look at itself and see if, among all of its assets, there lurk long-range liabilities. For example, the parish often inadvertently breaks up the family. It does this by having so many good things for individual members that it leaves no room for the family as family to grow. The parish has many fine adult education courses, but often only the women who do not work outside the home can attend. Or else the husband's travel prohibits him from taking advantage of the course offerings. The net result is that many women are becoming quite sophisticated theologically and spiritually and in the process widening the gap between themselves and their spouses. This may be the time for the parish to be flexible and reroute its impact. It may even decide, obviously after much soul searching and nervousness, to adopt Dolores Curran's suggestion that parishes suspend their usual religion classes for children and offerings for adults for a whole

year and deal *only* with family units. Declare a moratorium on educating the individual and concentrate on entire families (again, family being broad enough to include singles, young and old, widowed, one-parent families, etc).[4] Bold flexibility such as this gives testimony to the Spirit's constant ability to surprise us as it pushes the parish through the never ending process of the rhythms of death and life.[5]

There are many more ideas and community builders than its possible to list here. One simply has to pursue the parish trade journals and religious education publications. They consistently come up with engaging programs for families, classes, and parishes. There is no one formula that works for every parish and no formula that works all the time in the same place (parishes, like people go through infancy, childhood, adolescence, and old age and adjustments must be made accordingly). It is just that these are some approaches, some earnest thrusts in the large, uncertain, and challenging project of trying to build community out of disparate peoples, of trying to be the best sacrament possible. They are only human efforts but necessary ones. We must plant and water while awaiting the God-given increase (1 Cor 3:6).

As I close this chapter of pastoral postscripts a favorite saying comes to mind. It is from Pascal who said, "Everything starts out mystique and ends up politics." This is true even of religion. Christianity started out as an experience of a charismatic figure called Jesus and ended up with the politics of the institution. Yet for all of that the mystery remains. The figure of Jesus emerges renewal after renewal and has never been wholly suppressed in spite of our best and worst efforts. I think we are in one of those "distortion" times that will reveal his holy face more clearly again. I think that the parish, however transmuted, will have a large part in this revelation. I think, in short, that all our nonsense politics will give way again and again to the mystique of that love revealed fully in Jesus.

We are living in trying but exciting times. We are witnessing the slow but inevitable shift of the whole Western Christian axis to the southern continents. The church in general and the parish in particular are bound to be influenced by this cultural and spiritual realignment. This novel perspective of the gospel, coming as it does from the lands of dire want and need, may give us a new compassion, a new emphasis on the age-old message of salvation, a thirst for justice and mercy for the oppressed, a fresh sense of our common brotherhood. Whatever happens, there is a deep instinct that says more and more all of this will be absorbed by and move upwards from the grass roots. And by definition that is where the parish is. And, as long as I am able, I want to be a part of that.

3

What follows now in the remaining pages is a collection of suggestions that try to enflesh the principles we have discussed in this book. They need no explanations for they speak for themselves. It's a potpourri collection, but the careful reader will be able to read into them and work backwards to the principles they express. What is presented here is hardly the last word, for so many other parishes are so genuinely creative that we must learn from them. But as an appendix of notions and a catalogue of ideas and ideals they may offer some concrete direction and expressions for the reader who wants not only the theology but the application as well.

Notes for Chapter 10

1. I write from my own experience in lower and upper middle-class parishes. I know nothing first hand of the inner-city parishes, the struggles and aspirations of the minority parishes. I must learn from them. For a look there, see Richard J. Tlapa, *The New Apostles* (Franciscan Herald Press, 1977).

2. There are commercial bulletin fillers such as St. Anthony Messenger Press Updates and Dolores Curran's articles plus children's weekly scripture puzzles and games.

3. This was the whole thrust of my book, *A New Look At the Sacraments* (Fides/Claretian, 1977).

4. See Dolores Curran, "Family: A Catechetical Challenge for the Eighties," *The Living Light* 16, no. 3 (Fall 1979), pp. 364 ff.

5. Rhythm and flexibility necessarily include periodic soul searching on the part of even the effective pastor as to whether he should step aside for new blood, new vision, new leadership.

Appendix of Ideas, Tried and True

There are many suggestions for enlivening the parish spirit scattered throughout this book and they are easily extracted. Here I would list almost forty more of tried and true ones we have found helpful. The tried and untrue ones I'm not going to mention beyond the comment that we have our failures and blunders like the rest of the world. Some of these ideas are original, some borrowed from sources now lost to memory, some gathered from the professional parish and catechetical magazines. A few are repeated and expanded from the book. (Of course it should be remembered that what works in one parish destroys another.) With one or two exceptions I will not bother with our liturgies, the fine things we've done in preparing the whole parish to celebrate confirmation for example. There are too many books, articles, and programs these days that offer all kinds of exciting liturgical expressions for the parish. Nor will I mention the socials that are normally a part of every parish anyway. And finally, be it noted, that no amount of razzle-dazzle shadow will ever substitute for solid parish substance: good homilies, good liturgies, a good spirit, shared and trusted ministries on all levels, and full communication. Anyway, a list of some nearly forty ideas in no particular order of importance.

1. *The Parish Booklet.* Because we have so many activities and so many people from outside the parish boundaries who use our facilities, we found it expedient to put out a parish booklet each year. It's a standard 8¼″ × 5½″ production. First of all, the

parish booklet is titled with an annual theme around which, however obliquely, all parish groups are to revolve. For example, one year the theme for the parish was the "Year of Community" and all efforts were bent towards bringing that about. Other years have been titled the "Year of Faith" (big push on adult education and prayer), the "Year of the Spirit" (our first parish confirmation celebration), the "Year of Spiritual Renewal" (our first parish mission), the "Year of Vision," the "Year of Celebration," and so on. The booklet is divided into seven sections: committees and organizations, religious education, liturgy and spiritual life, parish social life, social affairs and services, a "What's new this year?" section, and a month by month calendar of parish events. We make up this booklet during the summer so that it is mailed to every family by Labor Day.

The parish booklet has proved very helpful in focusing our sense of direction and giving us a sense of purpose and common goals. It is also a handy compendium of information. Also, since we have so many activities we go out of our way each year to ask a Host Couple or Host Individual to oversee and run each affair. We ask different people each year to spread the responsibility around and to prevent the building up of cliques. Practically almost everyone accepts since the event is a one-shot deal and last year's host is on hand to encourage and help. People from almost every state in the union have asked for these booklets. If you are interested, write to us.

2. *Bulletin Stuffers.* This is very popular and we get many favorable comments here. Each weekend we insert articles of timely interest from magazines or newspapers into the bulletin. Many professional outfits even provide ready-made inserts such as Alt publications which send out Dolores Curran's columns and scriptural crossword puzzles or St. Anthony Messenger Press's *Update* series, or Claretian Publication's *Bringing Religion Home* or Concordia House's (Lutheran) inserts for children. Whatever you use, inserts in the Sunday bulletin are an efficient and attractive way for adult education.

3. *Overnight Retreats.* For our children in the fifth and sixth grades we have overnight retreats at the Parish House (rectory).

The kids bring their sleeping bags on Friday night and stay over till Saturday morning winding up with breakfast at McDonalds. The program is varied and geared to their needs: a combination of filmstrip showing and discussion, songs and prayer, discussion and games. The kids are filled with anticipation of pillow fights and talking all night long. We are filled with the hope that a friendly, pleasant association with the parish will move the feelings and attitudes of the children towards the church.

4. *Mini-Breakfasts.* On the last Sunday of every month after our heaviest Mass (10:30) we have a mini-breakfast in our parish hall: free coffee, milk, juice, donuts and buns for all. It's a great mixer. Each month a neighborhood section of the parish is host.

5. *Food Collection.* Also, on the last Sunday of every month we have a food collection at all the Masses. We put two tables on either side of the altar and people come to church bearing bags of food and paper products for the needy. We bring these over to the active open pantry run by our local Catholic Welfare Bureau.

6. *The Christmas Crib.* Like most parishes we too have a Christmas display. But we have a large one outdoors built by the Men's Guild with our Martha/Mary Guild buying the life-size figures. Sheep from a nearby farmer are penned in. The point is the public display, spotlighted at night and the cooperative effort that makes it possible.

7. *Keeping the Grounds.* We have a large property on which is our parish church and hall, the parish house, and now our new spiritual center. In addition, we have an outdoor St. Francis Meditation Garden. Family volunteers are responsible for various sections of the grounds—to keep it weeded, plant flowers, and generally maintain it. Parceling the work out this way gives a sense of communal pride and reduces our need to have a groundskeeper.

8. *Christmas Decorating.* At Christmas we bring in a large evergreen tree right inside the church—anywhere from sixteen to twenty feet high. But what is better is that each year we ask a different neighborhood group to decorate the tree and the en-

tire church. This policy not only spreads the work around more evenly and provides a friendly rivalry, but it also gives people a sense of being the church.

9. *Seasons & Children.* Two items here. On All Saints Day we have all the children come to church on the nearest Sunday wearing their Halloween costumes and saints costumes. Certain ones have had to research their namesake's lives and give a biography in place of the scripture readings that day. Likewise on Epiphany we ask the children to come to church dressed in the costume of their national origin. Also that day we hide three paper crowns under the pews and ask the children to get down on their knees to look for them. The three winners come up to the sanctuary where they are crowned, dressed in royal robes and sit there for the rest of the Mass. At the offertory they go and get the gifts.

10. *Passiontide Crosses.* We have asked fifteen families to make life-size crosses and stain them black. Then we erect them on our property during passiontide in ascending order up the hill. They are very striking silhouetted against the sky. On Good Friday, rain, snow, or shine, we make the outdoor stations at three o'clock using these crosses. More than a thousand people come every year for this moving devotion. After Easter the fifteenth cross is drapped with a white cloth. This could be done even in an inner city parish with crosses erected or painted along the streets.

11. *Lenten Stations.* On the Friday evenings of Lent we have families themselves conduct the stations of the cross in church. We offer them the various current versions or encourage them to write their own. It's up to them to decide who among them will do the leading, carry the cross and candles, and preach the sermon.

12. *Lenten Insert.* During Lent we ask people—adults, teens, children—to write a simple one-page Lenten meditation. We then use it as a bulletin insert for Sunday. The meditations are signed; the results at times have been quite moving and profound.

13. *Morning Office.* In order to train the people to the other legitimate forms of church worship, we introduced years ago the morning office in place of Mass. So on Wednesdays we have the office sung. This office is led by the people and among their number they choose those who will lead, read the scripture, and give a little homily. They distribute Communion after the Our Father. A nice and ancient variation.

14. *Christian Burial.* We made something of a stir, at least among the funeral industry, when we introduced our policy on funerals. We wrote a letter to all the parishioners (too long to reproduce here) urging them to a more Christian approach to death and burial and urging a more simple funeral style. This was done, not to undermine the various businesses, but simply in order to focus better on our gospel perspective. So we mentioned such things as: no flowers but the money given rather to charity, family cars in preference to limousines, and one-night wakes in the church rather than the funeral parlor. And a simple coffin. For those who so choose, the body is brought to the church on the evening before and placed in the center aisle, right in front of where we have our baptismal font—a great symbol of Paul's words (Rom 6:22ff). It remains there till the next morning's community Mass. We never have special, separate Masses for burial (or other occasions for that matter) if we can help it. We always try to celebrate special occasions before and with and in the usual community worship schedules. We also have a Lazarus Confraternity which provides hospitality for visitors. Our parish hall is attached to the church so bathrooms, chairs, and coffee are readily available. This policy has worked out beautifully and has impressed visitors. Best of all, it gives the tone we want: that people who have worshiped with us and who have died in faith are entitled to the joyous simplicities of the gospel. A side benefit of having the Mass at the normal morning community Mass is that the regular people are there to give tone, song, support to the liturgy—especially when there is a sizable group of visitors or non-Catholics who would need body language assistance.

15. *Welcome Wagon.* Like many parishes we have a group of people who once a month check out the township's tax rolls to see who the new people are and then pay them a visit, give them our parish booklet and make the first parish contact.

16. *Counseling Services.* A while back we made arrangements with our local branch of the Catholic Welfare Bureau to counsel our parishioners on a sliding scale basis. The arrangements are: we provide the office, the coffee, the cost of supervising the counselor, and any money differences the client can't pay. They supply professional counseling. It's a workable arrangement and mutually beneficial.

17. *Parish Trips.* One of the few socials mentioned here. We live near New York City, where many entertainments take place and to which we can bus easily. Every Christmas and Easter season we have a parish trip to see something. We buy block tickets at the lowest prices and make no profit by charging the people cost; but the spirit of this is worth the effort and people who could not otherwise afford to go on their own are appreciative. A good parish-building activity.

18. *College Newsletter.* Basically a out-of-sight-is-not-out-of-mind posture. We get the college addresses of all of our young parishioners and several times a year, in a large brown envelope, we send them a potpourri of parish bulletins, articles, and the list of all college students and their addresses. The College Newsletter is a touch from home and a sign that the parish cares.

19. *Alienated Catholics.* We have a meeting, several times a year, for those Catholics who feel alienated from the church for whatever reason. It is imperative to advertise by notices in other parish bulletins, the local newspapers, and radio spots. The turnout is good. We list major categories of complaints on a blackboard and then split up into groups. Experience has shown that three general categories predominate of alienated Catholics: (1) the divorced, separated, and remarried; (2) the traditionalists of all ages who are hurt by and dissatisfied with the changes, feeling betrayed by former "misplaced" loyalties to

the church; and (3) those who have run into insensitive clergy or religious. Just to listen, to be human, and not try to defend the indefensible are all that is needed to reduce the alienation.

20. *The Samaritans.* This is a group who have been through several courses such as Healing Life's Hurts or death and dying courses. They are now Samaritans, formally commissioned, who deal with needs, the sick, bringing Communion and in general the works of mercy.

21. *One-On-One Ministry.* This came about by accident. A few years ago a woman who had a mastectomy told me that, having gone through it both physically and emotionally, she would be glad to talk to any woman who was faced with the same problem. From this I began to ask various people who had and were suffering from other problems if they would be willing to do the same. Even more, would they allow their names and phone numbers to be put in the parish booklet? They would, and so in our one-to-one ministry we have people who know from personal experience: alcoholism, homosexuality, amputation, brain-damaged children, death of a child, cancer, job loss, heart attack, depression, divorce, chronic illness, and the like. These people are splendid "wounded healers."

22. *Church Bulletin Board.* In our church foyer we have put a large bulletin board for all kinds of public and church notices. It's a good focal point of interest. In fact, the notion is an offshoot of the old medieval cathedrals which were town centers and public information sources. Remember where Luther posted his ninety-five theses?

23. *Photos.* A picture is worth more than a thousand words. So inside our church, on the back wall, we have another smaller bulletin board where pictures of parishioners and parish activities are posted. The display is changed frequently and this spot forms a point of parish interest and gives a sense of identity.

24. *Advent/Lenten Packets.* Every year, just before the beginning of Advent and Lent, we send all the parishioners a brown envelope packet of all kinds of activities which will spiritually enhance these holy seasons. There is no end to the commercially

produced ideas, pamphlets, puzzles, activities that can be bought and/or reproduced for distribution. For those who use them, the contents are good spiritual exercises, good leads to the climax of Advent or Lent. We do include those old quarter and dime money folders but with the announced understanding that any money collected will go to this or that needy cause, not ourselves.

25. *Bible Vacation School.* We started this three years ago and it has proven to be a great success. We begin this right after regular school ends and hold it for two weeks in the mornings. There are many fine programs from both Protestant and Catholic sources. The casual and relaxed atmosphere makes it easy to learn. A consideration might be to have the Bible Vacation School jointly with a neighboring Protestant church (as we do here), sharing curriculum and teachers.

26. *Sunday Afternoon Movies.* So far in our township we have no movie house. So on some of the cold winter Sundays we provide movies (and babysitting) for a nominal fee. We usually show the Disney movies and draw the small fry. The kids are out in about two hours or so and everyone is happy—especially Mom and Dad. It's a public service.

27. *Blessing of Pets and/or Harvest.* Near St. Francis' feast day we ask the children to bring their pets to be blessed. And they do. Everything from gerbels to horses. Or else we have them bring ears of corn and such and gather around our St. Francis statue for a blessing of the harvest. Our St. Francis statue is a sitting one so that children can and do climb up into his lap and rest with his bronze arm around them.

28. *Easter Egg Hunt.* At all the Masses on Easter we ask the people to bring noisemakers to use as the Gloria is intoned. After Mass we have the grounds segregated for the various age group children to search for the Easter eggs. We have grown wise enough to use plastic eggs filled with jellybeans. It's not an improvement on Mother Nature, but it's an improvement for fresh Easter clothes.

29. *Saturday Night Dinners.* Every Saturday night I make dinner for a couple or several singles of the parish. We have a

standard letter of invitation which asks the people to come at 8:30 (which clears our 5:00 and 7:00 vigil Masses) for drinks and dinner at 9:00. I don't have a housekeeper so I've learned to cook tolerably well. This is a marvelous and revealing ice breaker. There is no better way to know people.

30. *Neighborhood Visitations.* About every three weeks, as scheduled in our parish booklet, we visit a home in one of the sections of the parish. The visit is informal and the host people ask in their neighbors, Catholic or not. It's a pleasant rap session during which we try to get feedback about the parish and the community. When we first began this we came in with a kind of Serendipity ice breakers but we found that this wasn't needed. Now we're more direct and ask outright leading questions and discussion starters.

31. *Moppet Masses.* The term, of course, comes from Notre Dame's delightful Father Griffin. On the last Sunday of every month at our 5:00 P.M. Mass we have this Moppet Mass. The children, prepared by their Religious Education teachers, do the readings, pantomime the gospel, bring up the offertory gifts and vestments (to which they attach homemade ornaments), decorate the church, and come up and sit around the celebrant in the sanctuary for a story-time homily. Afterwards there are refreshments in the hall, of course, and the inevitable balloons with our fun motto, "St. Mary's Parish, a community living and loving!"

32. *Big Rice Bowl.* Most parishes receive the little table cardboard rice bowls for Lent to put on their dinner tables. In addition to this we have had a large wood version of the Rice Bowl made and had it placed before the altar during Lent. As the people come to church they dump their little rice bowl money into the large one. Having the children do this is a special teachable moment. The big Rice Bowl also serves as a reminder.

33. *Staff Day Away.* We mentioned this in the book. The parish staff, workers and heads of organizations and parish council go away several times a year for a day of prayer, reflec-

tion, and then a good round-table sharing. Then it's to dinner for relaxation. These days test our vision and discernment.

34. *Pre-school.* On Sunday mornings, while parents are at the 10:30 Mass a group of qualified women teach a well organized and designed preschool program to the 3, 4, and 5 year olds. A worthwhile venture.

35. *Baptismal Letter.* Our baptisms take place, of course, at the community Mass. At the end, during the meditation time, I read reflectively the letter we give to the parents to be put away for the child; in fact the notation on the outside of the envelope has the child's name with the instruction, "To be Opened on your thirteenth birthday." A copy of the letter is given here:

Dear

Thirteen years ago your parents thought so much of you that they wanted to share the most precious gift they had: their faith.

So they approached the Christian community at St. Mary's, and asked the people if they would be willing to have a new member; and would they be willing to create a climate within which you could and would grow to know and love Jesus Christ.

The community said yes and so on   you and your parents and godparents and family and friends came to St. Mary's. There at the five o'clock Mass, in full view of the congregation you were inserted into the Christian family.

The people were happy and they applauded you afterwards. And then your parents brought you home and had a celebration there too because of this joyful event.

That was thirteen years ago. Now we hope that you have indeed been raised in the faith and know how much God loves you and how happy *he* was to have you as his child. For no matter what happens to you in life, no matter who hurts you, God will never stop loving you. Even when, like the rest of us, you make mistakes and sin.

Once he's set his heart on you he will never let you go. This he promised at your baptism. And God always keeps his word.

We hope therefore that this letter finds you well. Signing this are your pastor at that time, and your parents. The other names which you do not know are the names of people picked out from among the congregation who first formed your Christian family and first welcomed you into their midst.

All of us at that time gave you a hearty "welcome." Today as you read this thirteen years later, we still welcome you, pray for you, hope for you and—through the years and distance—love you.

Yours in Christ,

36. *Altar Breads.* Since there is a good trend to making a more substantial altar bread we have a group of both men and women who bake our large breads that the celebrant uses at Mass. They range from saucer size for daily liturgies to dinner plate size for the weekend liturgies. They are scored, easily broken and distributed and visible to the congregation. In short, the sacramental sign is very evident. There are several legitimate and approved recipes available. The bread bakers themselves feel more intimately a part of the Mass now, especially when their bread is used.

37. *Mail Slot.* Into the outside door of the parish office we have put a large mail slot. It is not only a handy place for dropping off papers and other communications, but it also serves as a permanent suggestion box. People are encouraged to use it in this way and to drop in complaints, suggestions, and just passing thoughts.

38. *Music.* Like most parishes we have a choir and the usual cantors. But we have expanded the music ministry to also include a traditional choir which sings at the monthly High Mass, a folk choir, the Moppet choir, and a parish band. We are not an especially musical area but we have enough good will and talent to create musically a nice atmosphere. Concerts, a variety show, and Christmas caroling enhance this atmosphere. "He who sings, prays twice," says St. Augustine. It seems we twice-pray a lot. Even at our daily liturgies.

39. *Associate Pastor.* This is not exactly an idea and not especially new but it is worth sharing that fact that my associate is a woman, a sister. I knew that when I was made pastor eight years

ago that I would never have another priest assigned with me. The parish (at that time) was too small and we were very short, and remain so, of male vocations to the priesthood. Therefore it meant that the people for a long, long time would have only one point of reference, one style of leadership. This meant that the people who did not like me, the ones I rubbed the wrong way or was unkind to, would have no other recourse. It was under these circumstances that I knew I had to seek another to work with me, to seek an alternative. Why not a woman with her view and grace and dimension that I would not possess? I consulted the people. For them, in the early seventies this was indeed a novelty. Wary but willing, they welcomed the first female associate pastor. We've had two in the eight years, the first one's illness forcing her to a different ministry. I must be candid and admit that the diocese still does not yet recognize her, but all the people do and our parish stationery carries her name as associate pastor. Eight years' experience has shown that a female associate is everything I had hoped the office would be. The people are pleased, and she has added a dimension to the parish which would otherwise be absent.

40. *The Final One.* Here, briefly, I would share one as yet untried idea for the parish that only time will verify. Over the past years, having struggled with the need for expansion, we finally moved from the notion of a sports-oriented parish center to the notion of a totally spiritual parish center. We listened to the growing voices calling out to God, we sensed the growing hunger for spirituality. Then we erected what we call our Christ House. Fundamentally it is a center, run by lay people, for lay spirituality. It is an experiment in parish spirituality. It's an attempt to blend the parish church and the spiritual center into an interrelating contact, one building upon and enhancing the other. The Christ House has an interesting design and includes a large all-purpose room, five classroom-type rooms, a chapel, two reconciliation rooms, a crisis room, a library dedicated strictly to biblical studies and spiritual reading, a multi-media room, two counseling rooms, a large conference room, and an office. Right now people are being sent away for

training (all volunteers) in spiritual direction, prayer group leaders, crisis room expertise, and the like. In this decade of the family we hope to have many family-related programs. It's a new idea and we are apprehensive about it; but the vision looks good and we're optimistic.